Resilience

A Story of Surviving Serious Medical Conditions and Living Life to The Fullest

Patricia J. Scott

Dedication

To my husband Karl, who supported my need to manage my illness my own way, and who was there to care for me, and rescue me when my body and spirit failed.

The discussions we have had while writing this book have given me a deeper understanding of his love and how this journey impacted his life. Particularly all the life changes he has made, as all caregivers do to support those of us who face life-threatening illnesses.

Karl married me while I was on the transplant waiting list without realizing how real the vow, *"In sickness and in health"* would be for the remainder of our lives. I am one very fortunate woman.

Acknowledgment

This book would have never been written except for the wonderful medical professionals at the University of Miami, Jackson Memorial Hospital and Indiana University Hospital who have kept me alive and healthy. Everything I am today is by the support of my family, and my friends, colleagues and the many students who stood by me as I experienced a roller-coaster of my continually unbalanced health and medical challenges, and the health professionals, transplant candidates, patients and recipients who shared their time and experiences to make my work possible.

I owe the ultimate accomplishment to my new friends at Roosevelt Publishing. Competently led by my editor, Breshkai Davis, and the production manager Dennis. The entire team was so patient with my continual rewrites, and general demands, Special thanks to James who was so helpful with the IT issues. Michael, Mark, and the rest of the team thank you. Breshkai, I cannot thank you enough for the long conversations and your insights on how to express my thoughts.

To Joanne, John, Michelle, Susan, Ann Marie, and especially Audrey and Karen for your generous time and thoughtful comments. I thank you.

And, mostly to my husband Karl, who has always been so supportive, who listened to me for hours, commented on drafts, and tolerated my head in the computer for the past year.

About the Author

Growing up in a small coastal town in the South of Boston, Patricia Scott was always doing something. As a child with two brothers and two sisters, she had no shortage of companions. She was a bright student involved in multiple school organizations and clubs, played in the school orchestra, and trained as a figure skater. Her ultimate career path as an occupational therapist was serendipitous as it embodies active engagement in society as a source of health and self-esteem.

As an occupational therapist, Dr. Scott treated people experiencing problems with role identification. However, in 1997, Dr. Scott's own role identification was threatened. She was told that she had a chronic liver disease. Over the next 15 years, her autoimmune hepatitis caused irreversible cirrhosis, and the only option left was liver transplantation. She did not want to be a patient or a 'sick' person, and most importantly, she did not know how. She scoured the research literature for information that would help her understand what her life would be like during and after transplantation. She found very little.

In this book, Patricia Scott shares her strategies, based on her experience as an occupational therapy researcher and academician that allowed her to live a successful and productive life. She describes how, in the face of two liver transplants, spinal cancer, a medically induced stroke, and complex autoimmune pneumonia, she earned a Ph.D. and became a celebrated teacher and an internationally recognized scholar.

The book is inspirational for those interested in learning about how one woman can accomplish wonders. It is about how this one woman refused to give in to a barrage of unwelcomed and unanticipated life events. It is also a story full of lessons about how to face uncertainty and say in the face of all the hurdles: *"I will not give up!"* Finally, this book will show how to fight the tempting dependency on the health care system.

Now retired as a Professor Emeritus from Indiana University, Patricia Scott is spending her time tying up loose ends with her research so that others can benefit from her findings, working to maintain health, and enjoying time with family and friends. Most importantly to her, she is spending precious time with her beloved husband and lifelong love, Karl Mann, at home and traveling the world.

A comment to Dr. Scott, during a hectic day on the Indiana Health Transplant unit from transplant surgeon, and then Head of Transplantation, Joe Tector, MD. Ph.D.:

"I can give them a new liver, but you can tell them how to live their lives."

Contents

Foreword

I have known Patricia Scott her entire life, and I have to say that from the beginning, as a child, she excelled in everything. She was a go-getter; she was a learner, a teacher, a positive influence, but mostly, Patty was an achiever.

When she was diagnosed with her life-threatening disorder, she took the news in stride. She jumped right into the fray, found out what she had to do, and was on top of the situation from the initial diagnosis. Her lifestyle changes helped her delay having a liver transplant for 15 years with diligence. Then, having gone through all of that, she developed cancer, had to go off her transplant medication, and after the chemotherapy, she had to once again wait almost to the point of dying for another liver.

During this time, she continued to work. She was a professor at the university. She continued to mentor students, she continued to learn as a student, and she managed the care of our disabled brother along with numerous other accomplishments.

She was just unstoppable, an amazing example of the will to live and how to do it.

Doctor Scott as I now call her (respectfully), has lived the past 40 years with unimaginable health challenges most people would not survive and she has done it with class, determination, professionalism, character, more determination, and most importantly, tremendous success

With incredible respect and love.

Joanne,

Sister to Patricia J Scott

"Before the beginning of great brilliance,

there must be chaos."

Prologue

Morocco is more beautiful, richer in culture and history than I could have ever imagined. We were on Day 4 of a 15-day small-group tour. There were 15 of us and a guide when we were called for an emergency meeting in the lobby of our gorgeous Riad in Fez around 11:00 PM in the evening.

"Morocco is closing all airports and borders as of 5:00 PM tomorrow," said our guide Rasheed. Have your suitcases outside your door at 7:00 AM. We will have breakfast and leave by 8:30.

When we left the United States on March 10, 2020, COVID-19 was a problem in China, Italy, and Iran. We flew through Lisbon, as we planned a seven day stay in Portugal following our Morocco tour. We awoke in our hotel in Lisbon to hear President Trump had closed all US airports to International flights. Two traveling companions were in-flight to Morocco when the pilot conveyed the news over the intercom. This was alarming as when we left the USA, and there were no travel restrictions or even warnings to our destinations. There were 3 cases in Morocco and 13 in

Portugal. Our travels put us in places safer than our homes in Indianapolis. Gate 1 Travel, our tour company, had over 250 travelers in Morocco, and their objective was to get us all out of the country safely. Meanwhile, all the hotels were closing, so they arranged for the Novotel in Casablanca to house us until we could be repatriated.

Turns out repatriation was not so easy....

Part I
Life before the Chaos
1953-1997

Chapter 1
The Beginning

My identity is all I have – the rest is outside my control.
I can control only what I believe.
I must hold on to myself or I may be gone
I am what I can hold on to.
I am me and then I am not.
Do not try to take me – I belong to no one outside myself.
Otherwise, surviving falls short of thriving."
-Patricia J. Scott

We are all exposed to the risk of illnesses, but not everyone experiences serious health problems. The trauma that a health crisis inflicts on you can leave you anxious and stressed. Facing the world every day can feel too hard of a task, and you can become frustrated and feel hopeless while experiencing the loss of your past healthy self. I have felt all of this because I have experienced it all.

Coping can be difficult, as everything reminds you that you are not the same person as you were before. You are at risk of feeling sorry for yourself, and your mind can easily convince you that everything has gone wrong in your life.

You cannot help but find yourself thinking about the person you were before the unfortunate diagnosis, and it can take a toll on you psychologically. You are at risk of identifying yourself with the illness and eventually losing your prior sense of self. You are obsessively aware that you are not the physically fit and emotionally strong individual that you were before the disease took hold of you.

When you sell yourself short, your self-esteem lowers, and you become unsure of who you are. It is frustrating because the physical pain, fatigue, and extra tasks associated with maintaining health can affect your routine life and your living space. You are not the same diligent and hardworking employee as before, regardless of your efforts. Others at home have to pick up the slack because of your fatigue and forgetfulness, and your friends wonder why you stopped keeping in touch.

The medication stuffed inside your bag and the symptoms which abruptly appear and disappear can stop you from completing any task with the same efficiency as in the past. Dealing with the doctor's appointments, lab tests, and taking your medicine regularly takes away a good chunk of your time. You also start to feel your body is getting weak, and you are continually tempted to give in to the couch rather than pushing all your boundaries and striving for the best outcomes.

The worst part is accepting that this battle has no end in sight. When you see others nonchalantly continuing with their lives, you are more aware of the burden you bear. They did not have to plan out their day according to how much energy and physical strength they would be left with by the end of it. All they require is to wake up fresh in the morning, grab their clean, crisp shirts, and continue with their professional and personal lives. Yet, there is you, starting to feel like you have to push yourself hard at each step to do what you used to do without such an ordeal. You are unsure of what will happen in the future, yet you have no choice but to keep moving forward. Your life has taken a turn for the worst, and you feel more challenged than ever.

I need you to remember that your illness should not bring you down so much that you feel less than others. When it came to my own illnesses, I convinced myself that I would never allow my deteriorating health to determine my worth. I would face every obstacle regardless of how painful it had been for me, both physically and mentally. I actively resisted negative self-talk or comparing myself to others. One solution was to select clothes carefully and intentionally look good. This often brought compliments that were very much welcomed. Another strategy was to answer questions from concerned others politely, and then change the subject to a topic more relevant to the encounter.

I found it important not to focus on my limitations and lack of physical energy and to remind myself I was still an extremely strong person, no matter how weak my illness made me. This is not simply a bluff, nor am I saying that because it feels right to say it. I truly mean it when I say, *every person suffering or dealing with a health condition is stronger than ever.* It is not easy experiencing pain, weight gain or loss, lack of patience, and gradual disinterest in things you once adored. Research shows that people with chronic illness are two to three times more likely to suffer from depression.[1]

If the negative thoughts in your head tug at you, remind yourself of people that love you and care about you, and

---

[1]Wilson-Genderson, M., Heid, A. R., & Pruchno, R. (2017). Onset of multiple chronic conditions and depressive symptoms: a life events perspective. Innovation in aging. Retrieved from:
https://academic.oup.com/innovateage/article/1/2/igx022/4638332

strive to do better for them. If you do not have such people in your life, reach out for help. You can join support groups or find a therapist to get through this tough phase of your life. Having someone who understands you and knows precisely what you are going through is important for your recovery.

When I talk about support systems or even just regular people you meet, I also want to communicate how not every person will offer you beneficial advice.

Know When to Take Advice

When you are suffering from a chronic illness, there is never a shortage of free advice on how to improve your health. This can be helpful and thoughtful, unsolicited advice can do more harm than good.

Even though the advice-giver means well, that does not make them an expert in your condition. People name supplements or recommend diets based on what they have read or experienced. Some people even insist on particular diets for reducing your symptoms. They do not, however, understand that everyone's journey is different. This is YOUR journey – you need to become the expert!

Most importantly, trust your instinct. When inundated with advice, it is important to keep the source and credibility of that source in mind. If the person who is offering you ways to improve your lifestyle is your physician, then you should listen intently. However, throughout the listening process, you must raise questions. The more you understand, the more you can discriminate. Filter advice, and keep what you consider would benefit you in mind. In the end, gather evidence and know who will give you healthful advice. Remember, you know best about your illness and condition because you are currently living and surviving it. Think about it: If you took everyone's advice, your head would be spinning from continuous change.

I discovered with time that success was related to trusting my inner self. Trusting your inner self means understanding which advice to consider, which to edit, and which deserves to be completely deleted.

Now that I extract only certain information from other people's words, I have been able to remove what is potentially unhelpful to me. It has been a life-savor. Instead of feeling overwhelmed by the immense amount of recommendations and ideas flowing in from all sides, I think of the source of the advice and whether the advice is suitable for me or not.

Learning to Live With My Illness

Though screening advice has been one of the best decisions I have made for my condition, another important decision was to become friends with my illness. It may sound unbelievable or even unachievable for now, but as the title of this chapter suggests, this is just the beginning.

The single most important step you can take is understanding your illness and learning to live with it. It is impossible to live a sane and comforting life if you keep denying the very thing that has become an unwelcome influence in your life.

Yes, your feelings towards your health predicament are valid. The sudden anger, frustration, and hopelessness are understandable and even acceptable. The mental strain of hoping to revert to the old days is common. However, I have learned one crucial thing from my illness; I must focus on survival. Do not allow feelings about your condition to control you. I realized the importance of acknowledging my condition but, at the same time, not giving it any authority over me.

Becoming friends with and accepting my illness does not mean I gave in to it. It simply means that I accepted my condition as a part of my existence and began to search for treatments and solutions to manage it before it consumed me. I started researching and analyzing my condition. I decided to participate in disease management instead of grieving over who I used to be or why this disease chose me. I am NOT a victim.

I learned there were certain things in my life I could actively manage. This included taking my medication on time, committing to a prescribed diet and exercise. I needed my body to cooperate with me, but it just was not complying, so I learned to adapt.

Some would consider my idea of acknowledging my illness yet not allowing it to take over my life to be just denial. In reality, I believe I am living a contradiction.

To understand this better, let's start with the basics. The dictionary definition of contradiction is "a combination of statements, ideas, or features of a situation which are opposed to one another[2]

I have a set of serious medical problems; I admit that. However, I do not consider myself a 'sick' person. My illness is outside of my sense of self, and I refuse to let it in. Honestly, I have to admit, it does sometimes take over.

Having contradictory thoughts about your illnesses is acceptable. You cannot stick to a straightforward way of thinking or just commit to the negative or positive. With chronic illness, a strict attitude and way of thinking can affect how well you deal with the illness. There is no guarantee of how your illness will play out every single day, week, or month.

There is no need to fixate on a single way of thinking. Just let yourself go and make room for contradiction. Basically, acknowledge and understand that your illness exists. You should know it is challenging, but remaining stuck on a single way of thinking can be harmful. So, let it all go and allow yourself some flexibility to adapt to the situation.

---

[2]."Lexico. (2020). Retrieved from:
https://www.lexico.com/definition/contradiction

As this book continues, you will find me talking about my illness and how it completely changed my life. I will look back at some of the times when nothing seemed to go well for me. I will reminisce about how I was once scared of my condition and the thought of experiencing organ transplant surgery. Slowly and surely, though, I learned to live with it, and I adjusted myself to the lifestyle laid out by my illness. Along the way, I started looking for information about life after transplant and found very little. Later, I devoted my time to conducting research about my recovery and educated myself by working with transplant candidates and recipients, which compels me to share with my readers what I have learned throughout the years.

In this book, I talk about how my illness consumed many years of my life, the heavy details surrounding it, and how it posed a huge challenge to me. I will share how I did not let it stop me from achieving my goals or prevent me from enjoying my life. You will also learn how my experiences as an occupational therapist helped me develop healthy habits and adjusted my course by making lifestyle changes. In the book, I will sometimes focus on a topic and talk about it over time, and in other chapters, I focus on a specific period of time. I recognize this can be confusing. Anyway Appendix A provides a chronological perspective on the events of my experience with illness and life today.

I hope this book, packed with my personal experiences of medical challenges and the transplants that saved my life, can help others face similar challenges. My thoughts are also informed by my research and interactions with many transplant candidates and recipients and their families, as well as health professionals. I hope it teaches you how to be brave even if you have not suffered from the same illness, do not fear your condition; learn to live with it. So, tighten your seat belts because this roller coaster of countless ups and downs is going to consume you for a while. It will make you think and feel things that you took for granted. Most importantly, it will teach you how just through a little courage, you can achieve wonders.

"Too many of us are not living our dreams because we are living our fears."

-Les Brown

Chapter 2
Who Is Patricia?

"Every time I stand before a beautiful beach, its waves seem to whisper to me: If you choose the simple things and find joy in nature's simple treasures, life and living need not be so hard."

-Psyche Roxas-Mendoza

This quote depicts exactly how I was brought up. It depicts the heart and soul of life with my mother. We were happiest with fresh air and saltwater and our toes in the sand. I learned to dance in the rain and fell in love with all the rainbow colors, and this is how I strive to live my life.

I do not want to suggest I grew up in an idyllic home where everything was cake and ice cream all the time. Life at 15 Pilgrim Road was as chaotic and unpredictable as it could possibly be.

Born in 1953, in Salem General Hospital, I was second in the line of five children; the eldest was my sister, Joanne. When I was born, we resided in Marblehead, Massachusetts. Salem, where the hospital was located, is well known for the

Salem witch trials, and my sister and I loved the association. Five months after my birth, we relocated to Hingham, Massachusetts, a small historic town 20 miles south of Boston. Hingham was chartered in 1635, and I lived on Pilgrim Road.

Although my story began with my birth, my family's inspiration came years before that. My ancestors had migrated to the USA from Ireland in the early 1800s at the time of the potato famine, and my mother grew up in Boston. My grandfather did well for himself and his family. He owned his own Electrical Contracting Company. He installed the lights on Mystic River Bridge in Boston, and the lights in Fenway Park home of the Boston Red Sox. It is cool to think Fenway had the first night games in 1947 with my grandfather's help. On June 13, they played their first game under the lights, recording a 5-3 win over the White Sox.

The Legacy of Survival

You may have heard many stories that people pass on to their children. These stories are legacies for the young generation that they can build upon in the future. These legacies aid people to hold on to what they believe in. With that knowledge, they can achieve just about anything. Some have tales of bravery. Some have struggled through poverty; my family has the legacy of surviving the odds. Whether it be my Irish ancestors who survived through the potato famine, my father, who fought tuberculosis for years or myself through my chronic ailments, we persisted, and not only that, we lived!

I am proud of the way everything unfolded in our lives, not only because we survived, but also because we came out better than we were before. Like a usual family, there were individual and family struggles. However, we gained the strength to face the worst. Through all the obstacles, we made the best of what we had. My grandfather's success in America was a living testament to that. He had given my mother strength, and she lived by two principles: *"if you work hard enough, you can achieve anything in this life,"* and *"If you do not have something nice to say, do not say anything at all."*

My mother's childhood was full of moments that she never forgot. She would tell me stories about how she sat beside my grandfather during baseball games. Her job was to count the lights that burned out in the park so his crew could replace them the next day. She really loved going to the games, sitting next to her father, and doing her job. This memory was not profound when she told me about it as a child, but now I realize that once we grow up, these little things add value to our lives.

In comparison to my mom, my father had a different background. He was from a blue-collar, working-class family residing in Rockland, Massachusetts. My paternal grandfather was a butcher. My father was a gifted sportsman. He excelled at basketball, football, and baseball. His skills earned him an athletic scholarship at Bowdoin College in Maine. Suddenly everything turned upside down when he was diagnosed with tuberculosis in the senior year of high school. His health deteriorated but, his will to live helped him survive two years, through agony and pain, in a sanatorium. Shortly after his recovery, he met my mother, and they were married in 1951.

Life slowly got into a rhythm, and everything fit into place, but not for long. Soon, after the birth of John, my middle brother, another challenge came to knock them down. My father lost both his parents, and my mother lost her father. Both my parents were in their early twenties at the time, and they lost three out of four parents. Their life was all tossed up, but they learned to swim when they started to drown. My surviving grandmother, God bless her soul, lived on until 96 years of age, and seeing her survive to this age has been a significant inspiration in my life. The conviction within her to live a long life and live it well will always be one of the greatest memories.

An Interesting Childhood

We lived in a suburban neighborhood. Our house was close to the Atlantic Ocean. Every summer, we would spend most of our time at the beach. Life tasted as if it was a mixture of all the amazing ice cream flavors out there. I would give all the credit to my mother for making me feel this way. She loved the beach. She had grown up spending her summers at the beach where she took swimming, sailing, and boating lessons. She had spent most of her time in the water. She had this philosophy that if you are facing tough times in life, just go to the ocean, and "the saltwater will cure everything." Although I now realize saltwater does not really work well when I was desperate to get back to health, it does put my soul at peace.

Little things in life and associated memories are what really help you get through some of the hard times in life. I cherished these moments always and believe it or not, they have brought me back from the verge of total hopelessness more times than I can count.

Growing up was amazing as we were five siblings, and the age gap among us is not much. We never had any problem finding someone to play with. Not to mention, there were a lot of children in our neighborhood. We used to gather every day, makeup stories, and invent games.

Our adventures were equal amounts of peace and peril, most playing with Barbies. However, one time, in particular, our game involved making a tent for our role-playing of an episode of *Little Women*. We used two lamps to prop up the sheet we were using to make the tent. Of course, we turned the lights on to see better. At one point, my mother called us for lunch, and afterward, we went outside to play.

Shortly thereafter, my mother called again, *"Girls – come in here"* in a tone that let us know we were in trouble. *"I went downstairs to do the laundry and smelled smoke," she said.* Needless to say, putting a sheet over an electric lamp was not a safe idea.

Some days, my mother would pick us up from school. *"Here get changed, we need to get to the beach while it is still high tide, you can change in the car," she used to say.* It was amazing how our lives revolved around high tide as Hingham was a harbor beach. Low tide = mud.

When it came to our educational grooming, my mother was very particular. She kept many books at home and made us read every day. When I was 12 or 13, she made me participate in a book reading contest at the local library where we got a free book if we won, and luckily I won. The book I chose as a prize was a Betty Crocker's Cookbook, which was quite interesting thinking about it now as I love baking. This involuntary participation really boosted my confidence. When I started college, my mother started working at our local library as a Children's Librarian. She needed a break from us kids she had raised at home. I have learned the best lessons of my life from her, and I will always owe her for that. I also still have that Betty Crocker cookbook.

Hands-on Everything

I was very curious as a child. I always looked for something to do. I remember a friend of mine, Aileen, who lived down the street with whom we re-enacted Broadway plays like Bye Bye Birdie and West Side Story. Another frequent activity was skating on Cushing Pond, in the frozen winter. By the time I started taking skating seriously, I was already ten years old, which is too late if you are looking to become a professional, but I did okay. I made my way further by taking proper lessons, getting formal qualifications by passing tests and later on, advanced to Ice Dancing.

My aunt, Sondra, taught me to sew. She was from Philadelphia, married to my father's brother, Uncle Dick. After learning how to sew, I sewed many of my ice skating costumes myself. At the time, I was really skinny, and at five feet and six inches, most of my body was legs.

I loved and enjoyed figure skating and ice dancing more than anything else I went to a certain point with ice skating, but it was not something I excelled in; it was an experience that taught me perseverance and made me realize the need to work hard in life. There was only one rule; if you fall while skating, no whining, no sympathy, just get up and do it again.

It gave me discipline, defined my posture, both mentally and physically. Skating helped me develop a strong sense of body control, particularly mastering my center of gravity, which later helped in skiing and so much more. In those days skating required figures and free style. Figures were proscribed patterns one had to complete through tracings on the ice. It was a very precise task and taught me about intense and focused concentration. I loved figures. Skating helped me in coping in later years. The lessons I grasped from it were both physical and mental.

The Teenage Years

In my teenage years, it felt as if I could spread my wings to the fullest. Everything seemed achievable and doable, except skiing. All my family could ski except me, but I was not allowed to ski because of skating. Everyone was concerned I would break my legs. I took part in everything. I recall my father saying, *"You never found a club that you did not join."* I was a good student, learning just came to me easily, but I never pushed myself for excellent grades. At school, I was more involved with things like spending time with friends and joining extracurricular clubs. I played violin in the school orchestra too, but soon enough realized that I was tone-deaf. I enjoyed other activities more. I remember theatre was fun also. I loved everything about the beach, swimming, and sailing as well as just hanging out. I even became a lifeguard as a summer job.

Just to explain my violin skills better, let me tell you something, we had a dog named Irish, which is a terrible name, to be honest. Whenever I played violin at home, he used to howl, and my brothers and sisters would leave the room the moment I began my practice. But, I had to try it, so I did.

Regardless of such an extensive involvement with everything, I have always been an introvert. Though I spent a lot of time with friends and took part in so many activities, I always needed time and space for myself. I remember doing silly things, such as standing on my head in the dining room corner. This one time I got so mad, I packed up my stuff, including my dolls, in two brown grocery bags and left the house. Looking back, I realize that both were clearly ploys to get attention. I did spend time with my friends, but I liked my space too.

After graduating from high school, I was all set to go to college. Before I went away to college, I came to a point when I needed to make some decisions. When my skating coach found out that I was preparing to apply for college, he got really upset and stopped giving me lessons. He always said one could not be a serious skater and attend college. He was convinced that most girls went to college to find a husband only. I told him I had no such intentions, and I would really like to make a career for myself, and it was not going to be in skating. I was persistent and went to practice regularly, and eventually, he gave in, but he still did not agree with me about going to college.

First Duel with Life

After clearing the air with my coach to some extent, it was time to choose what to study and from which college. A woman with whom I used to skate told me that her husband worked as a physiatrist at the Peter Bent Brigham Hospital in Boston. She knew I was unsure about what field of study to pursue, so she suggested I visit with him to observe physical, speech, and occupational therapy; she was convinced I would find it interesting.

I took her advice and went with him to the hospital. I went to a session of speech therapy first, and just as she had said, I found it quite interesting. Next, I went for a physical therapy session. I did realize its importance and the value it added in health care, but to be honest, I found it a bit too repetitive. The last one in the line was occupational therapy, and I was astounded by what I observed in this session. It was amazing. I completely understand and agree that every therapy is important, but occupational therapy was not a mainstream clinical interaction; it involved learning about each individual's needs and what is most important to them. And, assisting them to achieve it.

After this day, I knew what I wanted to become, but that was not all up to me. Before I could work on that, my father eliminated any college options inside a fifty-mile radius from home. He said that if I was going to college, I needed to go away, and he did not want my home every weekend, which eliminated all the schools in Boston, so the list shortened. So, playing on the safe side, I applied to four schools with four different majors. I applied for physics, mathematics, physical education, and occupational therapy. The initial plan was just to go wherever I would get accepted, but, surprisingly, I was granted admission in all the schools, and once again, I was back to square one.

I went for the occupational therapy major at the University of New Hampshire, and that proved to be the best possible decision I could have made. Occupational therapy has helped me a lot both in my career and in my personal life. I cannot imagine my life if I had chosen a different field.

Stepping Out of My Shell

I knew how important it was to survive at college, but I did not let that disrupt my enjoyment. I was stepping out of my small shell for the first time. I joined the college newspaper and became a photographer. I began skating again and participated in every other club I could get into. I did not want to spend my days in the library. I did want to graduate. I knew I could graduate with a 4.0, or I could graduate with the minimum 3.5. If I maintained a GPA of 3.5, just like the student with 4.0. I would still have the same degree, and I would still be an occupational therapist. Once admitted, I had to compete with fifty students for twenty-four available slots that was the tough part. Landing one of the available slots required a lot of survival skills, so I used them all and finally got through. For those of you who do not know, occupational therapy today lies among the top ten growing careers. The competition to get in is high. The route I took back then would not work today. I qualified to practice with a baccalaureate degree. Today, in 2020, some programs offer the Masters, but most prepare students to enter practice at the Doctoral level. In fact, up to the day I retired as a Professor of Occupational therapy, I had a sign on my door that says, *"No one really cares what your GPA was."*

This GPA did present problems later when I wanted to go to Graduate School. I was in Oklahoma, and I was an adjunct at Oklahoma University as I was teaching a few classes. Dr. Kathlyn (Kitty) Reed, the Chair of the Department, stepped in on my behalf and petitioned I be allowed to take courses on probation. The requirement was that I would earn a 3.0 in my first 15 hours, and I earned a 4.0.

Even with all the competition, I grew and matured at college. I tried so many new things and made some very special friends. Donna and Betty were among them. The three of us were seventeen when we first met and turned eighteen in October our freshman year. We turned twenty-one together, and next year we will have been friends for 50 years! I love these two; they embody the kind of friendships that transcend time.

Adulthood

Now, this was the real deal. College was about to end, and the exposure of real life that awaited was going to be exciting. Little did I know what wonderful opportunities and horrific challenges life had in store for me. Regardless, adulthood was here. It was time to get practical. After college, I had to do nine months of clinical internship. I planned to travel and explore other places during my internship. I was really looking forward to occupational therapy in mental health, so I saved it for last. My first internship was at a Pediatric hospital in Maine, then Moss Rehabilitation in Philadelphia. My third internship was at the University of Alabama, Birmingham.

I married my boyfriend, Steve, after my internships were over. At the time, it was 1976, and we moved to Virginia Beach where we lived until 1978, and shortly after we moved to Port Huron, Michigan. We lived there until 1979 and then relocated to Oklahoma City; I was twenty-six years old.

Suddenly, everything began to change. Initially, it was not very obvious as I had never faced any chronic health issues before. Just two years later, after we settled in Oklahoma City, reality hit me, and it hit pretty hard. During wellness testing at work in the early 1980s, I was found to have elevated liver enzymes. The confusing aspect was that I had felt nothing for a long time, no symptoms at all. I had been on my routine, running 3-4 miles every day. Life was as orderly as it could be, but it began to change. I started feeling odd; at times, I even felt as if I was hit by a truck, which was unusual for me.

Upside Down

With one diagnosis, my whole life transitioned into something entirely unpredictable. My whole world turned upside down. Everything I believed about my control over my body was gone. Up to this point, I believed I had control over my health. I believed that I was doing the best I can to maintain my health and fitness, and I was healthy as a horse, running a minimum of 40 minutes a day (by using minutes I can vary my route and not have to deal with miles). Nothing would go into my mouth unless it had nutritional value.

All the magnificent experiences that life had been bestowing upon me vanished, and now it was all about surviving. In instances like these, we learn that we do have a backbone and discover such capabilities that we could never have imagined we would possess. I could only cope with my situation because I accepted my reality and never quit.

I believe each of us has our life like a map, our body as a tool, and our experiences as training; how we use these assets is what makes our journey better or worse. Wherever we stand today, we did not get here simply because it was meant to be. It's because we directed ourselves here, and similarly, we are capable enough to get in or out of any plight. That is how I made through, and the choices I made are the definition of what I am and what I am capable of.

"I am not a product of my circumstances. I am a product of my decisions."

-Stephen Covey

Chapter 3
Prednisone

"Life is 10% what happens to me and 90% of how I react to it."

- Charles Swindoll

If there is one thing that I abide by and would pass on as a life lesson, it is the fact that each life event is only a small part of the overall. How you react to it makes your life whole. Being diagnosed with Chronic Active Non-A Non-B Hepatitis, as it was known in 1983, taught me that change in life is inevitable, and there is nothing I can do to stop it. There was nothing I did to get this and no-one to tell me what my life would end up like.

One thing about any change, good or bad, is that it is disruptive. If it is good, we experience happiness, elation, or shock. If the change is bad, we experience sadness, angst, or grief. It's how we cope with it after the initial reaction that matters. It depends on how we individually categorize it. Our vision plays a major role in how our life turns out at the end of the day. Your choice is to be a victim or a warrior; it is all in your control. My life took a huge turn when I was diagnosed. It was devastating in the beginning; I was confused. What would I do now? Will I be able to lead a normal life again? There were hundreds of such questions. I am no saint, and I had my fears and doubts, and I was frustrated by the lack of answers. Life stops for no one and goes on whether we allow it or not, and so I had to as well but with a change of direction.

In Oklahoma City in 1982, Dr. Larry Bookman, my first Hepatologist, came up with the initial diagnosis and explained to me what I was going through. I did some research on my own and talked to some of my colleagues and friends about my condition. I was in graduate school at the time and shared my medical records with a few fellow students, some of whom were MD's, others were biochemists. They were really concerned when they found out and did everything possible to help me understand what Chronic Active Non-A Non-B Hepatitis was. I learned a lot about my condition. It was amazing how concerned my fellow graduate students were, as I just had an acquaintance with them. We were on the same softball and soccer teams at the University of Oklahoma Graduate School. However, they did not really know who I was as a person outside the sports field and what was in my medical reports. Yet, they helped me cope with it. My diagnosis seemed like a roadblock in my life, but I had to learn to get over it and move forward, and the only way forward was...

Acceptance

It is rightly said that *you never know how strong you are until it is the only choice you have.* I was left with no choice but to accept my condition and move on. It was exactly like living with a whole new reality. It was hard to come to terms with the truth, but I had to accept it and move on. It became even harder when the doctor prescribed me Prednisone. Prednisone is an anti-inflammatory drug that is used to treat autoimmune diseases. Even after the diagnosis, I never felt sick regularly. I had periods of intense fatigue, and then everything would go back to normal. Initially, I was kept on a low dose of Prednisone. The side effects of the drug were not very severe. These side effects included just a mild increase in my appetite and mood swings. After the first cycle was completed, I felt much better. Afterward, my doctor agreed that I could get off of the medicine for the time being.

When I would get tired and listless, I knew my liver enzymes levels were rising again. I had no energy left in my body, and my concentration was gone. I would see Dr. Bookman and restart taking Prednisone, but this time with an increased dosage. The increase in dosage intensified the side effects. As soon as my lab reports showed that the liver enzyme levels had returned to normal, I was off the medicine again. The side effects, however, stayed longer.

I was on and off on the drug for 15 years. After a while, I had to start the drug with a much higher dosage than before. I also had to stay on it longer. This time the side effects were not only intense but very prominent too. My appetite increased a lot more than before, and I began gaining weight with each passing day. Prednisone undermines your natural immune response, and as a result, your body no longer needs to convert carbohydrates to energy on its own. It sends you the signal you need to eat and, at the same time, uses artificial energy from Prednisone as a primary source. Basically, all you eat is directly stored as fat and eventually makes you heavier. Your body gets old, you get puffy cheeks, and fat accumulates around your face and your upper back, which is unattractive.

All Puffed Up

Before Prednisone took over my body, I was in excellent physical shape. After one prolonged episode of Prednisone, I was very bloated. I remember my husband asking me, *"When did you blow up on me?"* This is a memorable moment. I was used to taking Prednisone by that time, and there was nothing I could do to avoid the side effects, so I accepted that fact. I had taken it for granted, and I would blow up and then return to normal. My inner self failed to match my outer self.

Blowing up was not really the worst part. Things got worse when I started growing facial hair, primarily on my upper lips. I do recall an incident. I was sitting with my occupational therapy staff one day, and one of them pointed out that there was something on my upper lip. Instantly, the others asked her to be quiet. I got up and went to the washroom to check and found out that I was growing a mustache. That's when I discovered waxing, which is painful, especially on the upper lip. Sometimes I even had to get other parts of my face waxed. It is an uncomfortable and rather unpleasant procedure.

Prednisone's side effects include moon face, excessive growth of hair on the whole body, acne, fungal infections, mood swings, and insomnia. I experienced most of these, however, I did not have fungal infection or acne at any point. Everything else on the menu was served to me. Prednisone is a drug no one should be on but, it will save your life when nothing else can. It's very contradictory, it does help you survive, but it is fatal in the long run. I have taken this medicine for so long now that I can identify anyone that is currently on it at one glance, that's how well I know what it does to your appearance. My nephews put it well to my sister Michelle. They would call her while Christmas shopping, and without any judgment, they would ask, *"Mom, are we shopping for our skinny Aunt Patty or our fat Aunt Patty?"*

Between Then and Now

The first seven years with the drug were not too bad as the dosage was low, and the effects were manageable. Over time, with higher doses, it changed me. I became very sensitive and would get easily offended with minor things. I said almost anything that came up in my head. Most of the time, I just stated the obvious, which was embarrassing. Nevertheless, I did have a lot of energy, and I felt hungry all the time. When you cannot do anything about it, then it's better to find what you can do with it. Try to find what seems even slightly positive; that's what I did. I used all that energy to run more and carry on with my life as normally as possible. My house was very clean and the laundry was done. And believe me, it's not a cure but, it does help.

Anyone who has been taking a high dose of steroids for a long time knows the struggle. You change physically and emotionally, and it takes a lot of hard work to get back to where you were. I continued to work which brought sanity to my life. I am sure if I did not work, I would drive the people I love insane. I needed my valued routines, the roles I treasured, that made me, ME. In my life, my health was part of the context. I was in control. I chose to react in a way that made me struggle, sometimes a lot, but it worked out well for me.

I was living in Miami when Hepatitis C was identified, so I was tested, and the results were negative. By that time, my condition was identified as Autoimmune Hepatitis. This meant that my immune system was destroying my liver. Autoimmune diseases occur when your body is fighting itself. There is a process going on in the body in which your immune system perceives a threat and retaliates. Due to this retaliation, the organs, in my case, my liver, became inflamed. Prednisone is known to be the best to manage autoimmune ailments as it is an anti-inflammatory drug. It reduced the inflammation and eventually turns the liver into scar tissues. The scar tissue accumulated and made my liver cirrhotic. Therefore, a liver transplant became essential for me to survive.

Prednisone is prescribed with two kinds of treatment cycles, one is to take it on and off, depending upon the symptoms, and the other kind is when you are consistently taking a managed dose as support. I researched both the types and discussed it with my hepatologist a number of times. It's my personal opinion and preference to take Prednisone on and off. Mind you, this was in the 1980s, and treatment has changed since then, and now involves a number of drugs.

Dr. Bookman had a huge influence on my life. One piece of advice he gave me that I will never forget, is 80% more, better. What he said was:

"You need to learn to expend 80% of the energy you used to. Plan on doing more, better."

Medrolling

Once I had a sufficient level of cirrhosis, my liver gave out, and that's when I had the first transplant in the year 1998. After the transplant, I was scheduled for another cycle of steroids; Prednisone and Medrol, which was of the same compound but different brands. When I was on a higher dose, my husband would tease me whenever I got sensitive or irritable by asking, *"Are you medrolling?"* and I would instantly realize what I was doing and would answer, *"Yes! I am medrolling."* His ability to use humor to deal with my irritability was one of the most important encouragements I had. It helped us both survive.

The Last Episode

Taking Prednisone on and off worked really well for me. I was able to put off liver failure for almost 15 years because of this method. The eventual transplant replaced my scarred liver, but I still had autoimmune hepatitis. Anti-rejection medications are taken after the transplant to suppress the immune system to prevent rejection, and as a result, they managed my autoimmune condition very effectively. Many people with suppressed immune systems get sick. Luckily, that is not the case with me. I do not get sick very often, but when I do, it's bad. Thankfully, though, it's rare. My last episode of Prednisone occurred in 2017 upon return from taking some of my occupational therapy graduate students on a service-learning trip to Belize.

At the end of the trip, we visited Caye Caulker, a coastal island off the mainland of Belize. The purpose of the trip was to process the experience with the sponsors and enjoy some relaxation before returning to the university. Some of us went snorkeling. I can swim and snorkel. So, I was really looking forward to this trip. At one point, I dove down. When surfacing, I cleared my snorkel. That's when I found out that I had not cleared it very well. As soon as I took a big breath, I had inhaled a bunch of seawater. This incident resulted in a serious case of cryptogenic organizing pneumonia, a rare autoimmune condition caused by inhalation of a foreign substance – at least that's the theory of how I got it.

We returned late November, and I was in and out of the hospital from mid- December until the end of January. I almost died in the hospital. The doctors at the hospital were convinced that it was either a viral, fungal, or bacterial pneumonia. They did everything they could to save me. There came a time when they thought I would not even survive the night until they gave me Prednisone. This was a terrible time. Within two days, however, I was out of the hospital. It took another six months before I recovered enough to get back to work full-time. Nonetheless, because of this condition's high reoccurrence rate, I was on a nine month tapering course of Prednisone. I experienced the most severe side effects ever.

Prednisone at Its Worst

During my recovery period, I went to the lab to get some blood tests done. Later, my liver transplant coordinator called me and asked me where I was; I told her I was at home. She asked me to get to the Emergency Department immediately and not to drive. She explained that my blood sugar level was five hundred. I did as she had asked, except for the driving part. The emergency department was a short distance away, and I felt fine. I went in and told them what she had told me, and in the very next moment, I was being rushed to a bed. I could not understand what was happening.

Of course, this was on a Friday. For the next two days, I had to return each day as my blood sugar levels never stabilized; they even got higher into the 600's. On Monday, I got in to see my Primary care physician, and the doctor told me that I had to take insulin shots four times a day and check my blood sugar regularly. I never had diabetes, so I knew this was Prednisone.

I had to take insulin shots for a year, and then I tapered off when my sugar level was in control. I was put on metformin. It took another year to get my blood sugar at a normal level. I was still recovering from pneumonia, my lungs were damaged, I had a full face, I was getting heavier every day, and now I had diabetes to deal with. It was a major struggle, not much fun, but I survived it.

Now, when I look at myself, with all the episodes of Prednisone, it all seems worth it. It made me stronger. This is what happens when you have the will to live and never give up. I now have a condition called bronchiectasis, which makes me more susceptible to lung infections. At last, testing my lungs function better than most women my age, according to the reports. Last October, I did several 8-9 kilometer hikes in the Saxon-Swiss Alps in Germany.

Even with all the trials that Prednisone put me through, it did help me live. I am stating this fact because I want you to know that the recovery through this drug may be excruciating, but it saves your life. One thing I did fail to mention is Prednisone is very hard on your bones. I have had osteopenia (early osteoporosis) for many years, and just this last year, I was diagnosed with osteoporosis.

I realized that I had no control over how my autoimmune hepatitis impacts me—it has a life if its own, yet I could control how I react to it. So, I did what I could. What I could do was to drink a lot of water, reduce salt intake, follow a healthy diet, and get plenty of exercise. I already did all of those from the start, so I just had to keep at it. Eventually, I made it through successfully. People have always complimented me on how I handled myself during my illness. A good friend and colleague, Dr. Ann-Marie Potter describes:

"You were always so matter of fact and calm about your life. You would talk about your illness, your transplant, and even your cancer so calmly. It always amazed me."

The disease became a part of my routine. I accepted it, and what it was doing to me, I never considered myself a victim. I knew I had to keep myself under control. Just as everything else, Prednisone and its effects were inevitable, but I was determined to manage them, and I did the best I could. It is really important to take Prednisone as per the dosage. Otherwise, you can go into adrenocortical shock.

Over a long period, Prednisone suppresses the adrenaline system, and it becomes the primary source that the body uses for energy. You can taper it down until the system kicks in once again, but, you cannot immediately stop. Once you start tapering down, you will feel lethargic. It takes time for the adrenaline system to produce an adequate amount of cortisol to supply your body with the energy needed to carry out processes naturally. I run into a lot of people that are going through the same situation. It's a duel between body and mind. Your mind wants you to relax while your body has so much energy from the Prednisone inside.

At the time, prior to a lecture, I had to over-prepare myself and put a leash on my impulses. It was so easy to go off-script. It was a battle every time I needed to lecture within a certain time frame. I was distractible by nature. I loved to tell clinical stories, and I have a lot of them. My students always knew they could get me off topic, and believe me they did. I had to keep myself in check.

Love-Hate Relationship

Prednisone did make my life miserable over the years, but it also saved my life more times than I can count. I have a love-hate relationship with it. As I stated, I now have osteoporosis, which means Prednisone messed with my bones. I had diabetes, and it took two years to get my life back on track. I still take metformin, which is acceptable; insulin shots were not. I had to go through all of that because of Prednisone.

I took my insulin shots through the stomach; it's one of the parts of the body where it is allowed. I preferred stomach shots because there was an area on my stomach that was devoid of all sensation due to the number of incisions I had had over the years. It had been a kind of a silver lining for me. The art of surviving is to find that silver lining, and put your energy into purposeful and meaningful things in life, to take part in the things that matter to you – things you value. It can be your family, friends, spouse, work, parents, or maybe even numb areas of your belly where you can take insulin shots. Seriously, find something that you like to do, something which diverts your mind for a while. Take on whatever works for you.

If death is in the cards, it's here, and there is little to nothing you can do about it. But, even with so much happening, you can always choose how to lead your life. Live your life in a way that leaves no regrets. Time does not stop. If you confine yourself and stop living, you still lose this time. You would not get it back even if you survive. Death is unavoidable; everybody has to face it one day; no one has a choice. But surviving is a choice you can make every day.

> *"Some people are always grumbling because roses have thorns; I am thankful that thorns have roses."*
>
> **-Alphonse Karr**

Chapter 4
Karl

Commendable Vigilance

Written for Karl and everyone who supports Patty

A love tested true, from an outsider's view,
Endureth them much, strengthen both hearts,
To know someone's there, that they grieve, that they care,
Faith made of stone, never leaves them alone.
Open minds, healing hands,
Form miraculous plans,
The surgeons installing, doing God's highest calling,
Their hopes and their light, precariously thin many a night.
Blood through their veins,
Bears the brunt of many stains,
Emotions run high, now they try not to cry,
There's incredible strife,
When one fights for another one's life,
Yet the storms that they weather
Weave them closer together

-John Charles Scott Jr.

Love is not about showing affection when things are going well; it's about staying powerful when things are not. It is quite easy telling people that you love them but, walking with them through times when it's not just hard but brutal is a whole different thing. As I said before, in a really bad situation, it is easy to forget the good things that are around us. However, awareness of the good times actually motivates us through the hard times, even if we do not realize it. For me, that blue sky was Karl, my husband.

Born and brought up in Germany, Karl is a good-looking man with a very slight but wonderfully noticeable accent. Karl worked in the foreign services back in Germany, which is equivalent to the state department here in the US. He served in Edinburg, Scotland, and Baghdad, Iraq. Then he ended up in New York at the German Mission to the United Nations and worked for three years until being assigned to Bangkok, Thailand, for a couple of years until he returned to New York.

The Beginning of Us

Just like me, Karl was married before. The marriage did not work out. However, he was already a US citizen; lucky me. When I met him for the first time, he managed a fine dining restaurant in Key West, Florida. I was there with a friend. At the time, taking Karl's word for it, I was an attractive woman with a really nice body and brains! That is when our friendship began, and later it turned into a happy relationship. Karl did not like the 4-hour distance in our relationship, but I could not move as I was teaching at Florida International University in Miami. So, he moved to Miami, and that's when we started living together. We had a townhome in Coconut Grove, Florida. We both still loved the Florida Keys and visited there often.

Since the beginning, we have had an extraordinary relationship. I wonder how I could have made it without him. I met him at a point in life when the last thing I was interested in was a romantic relationship. I had just gotten a divorce. I was not interested in this at all. Karl and I became friends and stayed that way for a very long time until we got involved. I think that helped our relationship to become stronger.

Later I understood that he was interested in having more than a friendship earlier in our relationship but respected my need for space. Karl has impressed me a lot over the years. A good looking man with a German accent is obviously appealing. He is very dignified and culturally sophisticated. He is someone who is equally comfortable in a tuxedo as he is in flip flops and shorts. He is comfortable and confident with himself in any environment.

Roadside Question

We decided to take a trip to Europe together. Before the trip, we were in the car heading to a sunset cruise in Key West. I was driving. Suddenly he asked if we were going on this trip as a couple or just as friends. I was stunned. He took me by surprise, and I pulled the car over to the side. I did not know what to say. I asked for some time to think about it. I had the same reaction when he proposed to me; I did not know what to say – and those who know me will tell you I am rarely speechless. I was wondering when he would ask me to marry him, but he caught me off guard. Those two incidents were six years apart.

Karl has been so kind to me, and due to my need for care has given up so much of his own life and professional goals. Although he has done very well for himself, he had to interrupt his career several times. Neither of us had family in Miami. Karl's entire family lived in Germany, and mine was several states away. Although they did come to Miami, my family could not be there all the time when he needed help or support.

On One Knee

My sickness was developing, and the visits to doctors and the hospital were just routine when we started living together. Karl did not know much about my autoimmune hepatitis and how it affected me. After six years of our relationship, in 1996 in Germany, he proposed to me. It was wonderful, but more about that later.

In 1996, I had the dissertation for my Ph.D. to complete. At that time, my father had been sick for a long time. Both of these events put marriage on the back burner. This was a lot to handle with working full-time, yet the real problem began when my doctor asked us to consider a liver transplant. For me, that was pretty shocking, but it was a real wake up call for Karl. He was confused, but the doctor said that a transplant was essential. Karl had so many questions, and we had so many discussions over my illness. Previously routine hospital visits suddenly turned into a matter of survival. He had no idea what was happening and what he could do to fix it.

Karl is precise about things; he likes to know what is happening and the potential consequences and to keep himself well prepared. If things do not go as he predicts, he can get pretty stressed. Stressing is what he calls it. This was exactly the situation where no one could be a hundred percent certain about what can happen, but not even once did I see him become aggravated. He was always calm with me, knowing this was just as stressful for me as it was for him. He suppressed his own feelings and prioritized me. I have thought about this situation a lot and how it reflects how much he loves me. I am incredibly lucky to have this man in my life, and I hope that if the situation presents itself, I will be half the person he was for me

Awestruck

One day Karl came up to me and said that he wanted to get married before the transplant. I started to disagree, and he responded, *"as a boyfriend, I have no rights. If you need me to make some decisions for you, if I need to help, I may not be able to."* He made it sound so simple and easy. Statistics show how many marriages fail when faced with serious illness, and this man wanted to get married to me as soon as possible. It was an awestruck moment.

The Call

When the hospital called me in for a transplant, we rushed there as soon as possible. A couple of our friends were there waiting at the hospital, Michelle Adams, my maid of honor, and John, a friend of Karl's. After I was admitted and taken to the operating room, Karl told our friends to leave, which was appalling to them. He told them that he was going home and wanted to be alone for a while. This was his way of coping up with the situation; it was not easy for him.

Longest Night

The head of the transplant team had told Karl not to worry and asked him to go home, but obviously, there was no possibility his mind could be at peace. The doctor told him that he would call in the morning or in the middle of the night to inform him how it went. It was a very lonely night for Karl. Through the night, he prayed and cuddled with our two cats. He called them his best friends. One of the cats was named Zeller Schwartz Katz after the German wine, Zeller, for short, and she was smarter than anything we had seen before, she could pick up on one's feelings.

The nightmare came to an end when the doctor called him and told him that the transplant went well. Karl was asked to get to the hospital at ten in the morning, and as soon as he got there, I was rolled out of the operation room. Because of all the effort that I had done previously to maintain my health, I had a pretty speedy recovery and was out of the hospital in just seven days.

Karl had a small digital camera, and while I was in the hospital, he took pictures every time he visited. This was 1998, way before the internet was in common use. He created a bulletin board online and would post the pictures there so that our family and friends were updated about my recovery. It was initially a way to cut down on the number of phone calls. However, a benefit was that he got a great deal of support and encouragement, which he needed at the time. Every day he would print out the messages and read them to me when he came in. I vividly remember the early days when I was really sick, and it was hard to process what he was saying. I was glad he was there, but I was unable to muster the energy to show enthusiasm. I recall trying to be excited, but it was so hard. Later on, it became a highlight of my day. Recently I looked again at these messages, and I got a kick out of reading them. So many wonderful messages from my FIU colleagues and students, family, and friends. It was so early in the days of the internet one person said this was their first email ever!

By doing this, Karl protected me from phone calls and visitors. This experience reflects how important I feel about allowing a sick person to be sick. I always appreciated that Karl came for several short visits every day. Sometimes he would bring a book and sit there and read. This was better than asking me to be active and excited for extended periods of time. It is incredible how much energy it takes to entertain company or even show enthusiasm when recovering from major surgery. Being in the hospital is hard work.

Short-lived Recovery

After I was home, it was within six weeks or so when I started having problems with my bile duct. Eventually, they inserted a tube (a catheter) between my ribs and later into my chest. The tube they inserted needed to be drained and cleaned daily, sometimes twice in a day, especially after taking a shower, and Karl did it. The first time when he cleaned and dressed the wound, we were both very nervous and essentially unprepared, but a week later, he would tell me to hurry so that he could clean up and dress the drainage area. He learned quickly. It all became a routine, and the way he adapted to the circumstances was amazing. He never complained or whined about how hard his life had become or what he had sacrificed. I sometimes felt guilty, but I was so sick that there was nothing I cared to do about it. In such a state of health, it is natural for a person to become so self-centered they are insensitive to the demands they make of their loved ones.

Preparing for the Worst

We had just gotten adjusted to a routine when another lightning bolt struck our lives: I had a stroke. The hospital reached Karl and asked him to come over as soon as possible; I was already there. As soon as he arrived at the ICU, a doctor asked him if he had seen me yet. "No," he said. The doctor responded, *"You need to know we do not expect much."* Karl was shocked. One of the transplant coordinators was there and told him she would take him to see me. She did her best to comfort him, but he was overwhelmed when he saw me. I had a distorted face, my lip was hanging down, and I could not speak. I cannot imagine what he was going through at the time. I was on a ventilator; I have no recall of the early time after my stroke, so there was nothing I could do to help.

Luckily, I recovered in four weeks; the only problems that still plague me are balance problem, a slight foot drop (which makes me stumble), and handwriting difficulties (problematic to start with but now awful!).

As I mentioned, people in my position become so self-indulgent, we are totally absorbed in our pain and anguish. It is obvious that we are suffering, but so are our loved ones. The mental pressure that builds, the helplessness, the trauma, and every day they gather strength to fight with it. My point is that our life was all about me, and even though I was in so much pain, it was evident that he was in no less. His helplessness was overwhelming, but he never backed down; he never showed it to me.

CHOP

One after the other, it was like life just waited to beat us down even before we got up completely. I started having back pains. After suffering from it for several months, doctors found a tumor in my L4-L5 vertebrae, and I was diagnosed with non-Hodgkin's spinal lymphoma. The CHOP[3] chemo was torture; it reduced my state of health instead of improving. The chemo would have killed me if I had continued on this therapy. After the chemo was stopped, I was kept on radiation only. The risk to die did decrease, but the experience was not any less terrible. I went through a loss of hair and weight. This was a discouraging stage. Hospitals became our second home, and Karl became a full-time caregiver.

He gave up everything during that time for me. All his ambitions, goals, and professional life was kept aside, and he says he does not regret giving up his ambitions to take care of me.

Getting Along

My family and Karl got along well. They supported him and were there when we both were struggling through my illness. Karl loves my sisters; they came to visit during my transplants, and then when I was sick with cancer. Joanne

---

[3] cyclophosphamide, doxorubicin, vincristine, and prednisone, a potent chemotherapy cocktail

lived in Ann Arbor, Michigan, at the time, Michelle in Hilton Head, South Carolina. Coming to help was not easy, and Karl knew they would like to be there more than they could with work, family, and life demands of their own. He did call when he was at his wits' end. One example was when I was going through CHOP, the chemotherapy I required for my spinal cancer. I recall being at Sylvester cancer center, ready for discharge, and Michelle walked in with Karl. *"What the hell are you doing here?"* was my greeting. I was very glad to see her.

Before they arrived, I had taken a shower, and my long dark curly hair started falling out. For someone who has never experienced hair loss with chemotherapy, it is nothing like you would expect. The hair literally lifts off your head. No sensation at all. When they arrived, I was sitting in bed, running my hands gently through my hair, and putting it into a large zip lock bag. After seeing what I was doing, Michelle remarked, *"And what exactly do you plan to save that for?"* I realized how useless the hair in the plastic bag was. Anyone who has had the experience of losing hair from chemotherapy will tell you, it is not like one day you have hair, and the next day you are bald. It comes out in clumps and patches.

On the way home, I expressed a desire to get it buzzed. We called David, my wonderful long-time hairdresser. He told us to come down right away. When he saw me, I could see him getting teary. As he ran clippers to remove my remaining locks, he was crying, and Michelle was crying, too. I pleaded them to stop as it was all I could do to maintain my composure.

Michelle was a good companion to Karl. They enjoyed each other's company and had many laughs. Michelle, being the youngest of the sisters, was fun to tease, and she was a good sport about it. She is also a very kind and sensitive person and the peacemaker in the family. I love her for that. She had a difficult time seeing me so sick and desperately wanted to make me feel better. These were hard times, and they took a toll on her.

An example was the time during chemotherapy when I was throwing up all the time. My sister just wanted to help me, and Karl explained I preferred to be alone when I was so miserable. He read me so well; he just knew what I wanted. At the same time, however, Michelle was a trooper, and her support was important to Karl and to me.

Joanne, my older sister, is very different. From an early age, she had learned to be the strong one. She was a pragmatist and looked for the things she could do to make a difference and do what she could to help Karl while not getting in his way.

Like Michelle, Joanne has a great sense of humor. She was visiting one time when it was my birthday, and I was in the hospital. A friend and colleague, Dr. Susan Kaplan, had come by with presents and balloons, including a bag of really nice-looking chocolate chip cookies. At the time, I was having trouble eating anything, to the point where they were threatening to insert a feeding tube if I did not start eating. After a period, Joanne asked, *"Are you planning to eat those cookies? I'd hate to see them go to waste."* I love Joanne. I also recall how, later that day, my friend Kathy came by. Kathy and Joanne knew each other well from growing up and had not seen each other for 20+ years. I am not sure how the events unfolded, but Kathy offered to bring Joanne back from the hospital later that day, and I noticed the relief on Karl's face. It occurred to me how little opportunity he had to be able to have some time by himself, knowing I was in good hands. It escaped me prior to that how exhausted he was. Sisters are like angels; they know when they are needed. My friends are awesome, and they know when I need company and when I need to be left alone. I could not do without them, and Karl could not.

Gilder Radner's Cancer House

During cancer treatment, I was growing weaker every day. I hardly ate as I had sores in my mouth, and Karl would beg me to eat just a little bit. I lost so much weight; it dropped down to 104 pounds, which was not much on my 5'6" frame. I had no appetite, and the sores hurt whenever I tried to eat or drink.

As the medicines took their time, we found other ways to find comfort. In the past, transplant support groups helped us, so we started attending Gilder Radner's Cancer House. I would attend a group with the other people who had cancer while Karl sat in a group with their caregivers and family members. After hearing the stories from the family members, Karl expressed his preference to go through another transplant rather than cancer. Unfortunately, his preference soon turned into reality.

Due to the cancer treatment, I had to stop taking anti-rejection medications. This made my liver suffer, and another liver transplant became imperative for me to live. The second transplant was a bigger risk than the first. I was already suffering from cancer, and my decreased health reduced my chances of survival. We had to wait longer than before to find a match: 6 months rather than 6 weeks.

The Pilot Program

While we were waiting for a match, our transplant coordinator asked us to come down to the Jackson Memorial Hospital at the University of Miami. Producers who were filming a pilot for A&E Television wanted to meet us. They wanted to hear our story, so we went there. After hearing us, they were amazed by all that we went through and asked if we would participate in the pilot program, and we agreed. We supported anything to promote awareness of organ donation. They were supposed to come to our house for the interview and filming over the next few days.

Karl was working nights, and I was just plain exhausted, so when we got home, we went right in for a nap. That is when we got a call from the producer. He told Karl that he had talked to the Chicago office, and they were going to start filming right away.[4] Their crew was already on its way to our house. They came and started to work. While they were filming, my phone rang; it was the transplant coordinator. They asked us to get to the hospital within three hours as they had a matching liver. As it turned out, the film crew knew the call was coming, so they took advantage of the situation.

Karl was really worried because they gave us a three-hour deadline to arrive at the hospital, and it would take an hour just to complete the formalities at admissions. Fortunately, we had a camera crew behind us at the hospital, and because of that, an hour's work was done within ten minutes. I was taken to the operating room, and after another long night, Karl and I both had a lot more in store. The second transplant was difficult, and instead of being in ICU for 24 hours, I was in over a week. I went back into surgery twice to control

---

[4] An excerpt from the filming is posted on the website for this book under the heading 'Liver Transplantation'. It was filmed out of Tower productions in Chicago.

internal bleeding, and with all factors combined, the recovery time was much longer and much more difficult.

The Man I Married

My husband has been the best husband and best caregiver I could ask for. Even after losing so much time and so many opportunities, he says he does not regret any part of it. If you ask him today if he would do it all over again, if he had a choice, he still says that he would. I was determined to come out of that situation, and he always believed in me. We did make it and returned to our lives. Karl returned to the wine import business and me as a professor of occupational therapy.

In his role, we visited Germany and the vineyards in Chile, Argentina, Italy, Spain, France, Australia, and New Zealand. In the last five years, he opened and has been the managing partner for a restaurant/brewery in a restored church until he was diagnosed with cancer. He had prostate cancer, and he successfully recovered after the tumor was removed. Unfortunately, a few weeks later, he developed an infection and became septic. He was seriously ill in the hospital for a week and took stock of his life during that time.

This was a role reversal, and I was the one who stood by his bedside and took care of him. It was an eye-opening role reversal for him. He was 66 years of age and working between 60 and 80 hours per week. When he returned to the restaurant, he informed his partners he was planning to retire in six months.

Karl has always been there for me. He somehow always knew what I needed and when I needed it. I do not know if I would have made it to this point without him. What I find amazing is that the thought of escaping never occurred to him; in fact, he says that all these experiences have made him more spiritual. Once, needing some spiritual fortitude, he ended up going to a church and found that it was locked. He knocked on the door, and someone came and told him that it was closed, to which he responded, *"How could God lock his house to people in need."* He ended up going to a different church.

After the second transplant, it was much more difficult than the first time to regain my strength. Everyone who knew Karl was aware of his independent nature. The way he owned the situation and took accountability for my every little need really made me feel positive and strengthened my will to survive. There were moments when I would get cranky and edgy, but we both never lost hope.

If I had a Chance

If I had a chance and knew beforehand what was going to happen, I would never put him through all of that again. I would not put anyone through that. I never asked Karl to give up his life for me, but it all ended up in a situation where he did what I would never ask any human being to do. I am more than blessed to have this man as my husband. He has given me more than I could imagine. I have gone through a lot in my life, but there can be no better reward for me than the man I have as my husband. He never failed to understand me; I had his attention when I wanted, and he gave me space when I needed it.

We both are retired now and are currently looking to cross things off our bucket list. We went to South Africa, Paris and spent a month in Italy. We recently came back from Saxony, Germany, and now we are planning to make a trip to Morocco and Portugal soon. We have prospered together and came a long way. We look forward to a lifetime together.

It is my goal to give Karl the attention, care, and love that he has flooded me with through our time together.

"True love is inexhaustible; the more you give, the more you have. And if you go to draw at the true fountainhead, the more water you draw, the more abundant is its flow."

-Antoine de Saint-Exupery

Chapter 5
1997- You Have to Do, What You Have to Do

Life is a continuous series of unpredictable events and surprises that are sometimes so beautiful and overwhelming that they become too much to handle. The rest of the time, they sneak the life out of you. That is why they say you must be prepared for the worst. Whatever this surprise is, it changes you. You can never be the same person that you were before that one thing happened, but what matters the most is your attitude towards it, and how you deal with it. The way you view the event is the basis of how your life is going to be. In 1997, there were many significant events...

Early in 1997

Karl proposed to me when I was least expecting it; I was surprised and somewhat shocked. We were in his hometown in Tirschenreuth, Germany. Everybody was glad to see Karl home, and they were aware that I was his girlfriend. The time and everything else was the perfect setting, as if the entire universe was helping him win my heart. I was in disbelief, but at the same time, I was on cloud nine. It was New Year's Eve or 'Sylvester' as it is locally known, and we were at a community celebration along with his whole family. Everyone was dancing the waltz, which is a typical way to celebrate in the region. Karl insisted that I dance, but I responded, saying, *"Karl, I do not know how to do it."* *"Relax! Just follow me, and I will tell you what to do,"* is all he said. I was tripping over my feet and very self-conscious, as I felt everyone was watching me.

At the time, Karl and I had been together for three years as a couple, and we had known each other for six. I had been wondering for quite a while now about Karl asking me to marry him. But, at the same time, I had been married before, and I did not think that I necessarily needed to get married again. It was like one moment I wanted him to propose to me, but on the other hand, I was ambivalent about it.

Being the center of attention at the celebration, I had no idea what was about to happen. I was shocked but awed at the same time. I was so into the moment and got involved in my thoughts he had to ask me three times before I answered.

Even with all the confusion and bewilderment, I said yes, and it turned out to be the best decision of my life.

After that, we went back to Miami, and on the way, we connected from Munich to Boston, and I got off in Boston to visit my family. Karl flew on Key West. I told my parents about the proposal, and they were equally excited, and at the same time, they did not want me to neglect my Ph.D. studies to plan for a wedding. Therefore, once I returned to Miami, I knew I needed to put all my focus on my dissertation. I was scheduled to graduate in the fall of 1996. Yet, I was still struggling to put together the final details.

The Beginning of Hepatic Encephalopathy

Today when I think about it, I know that it was the beginning of hepatic encephalopathy or HE as I will refer to it, but I did not know it back then. It is easy to look back and realize why I was more disorganized than usual and why I was having trouble putting ideas together, but back then, I was clueless. The HE was compounded by the high dosage of Prednisone I was taking as one of the side effects is difficulty concentrating.

Hepatic encephalopathy– Stage One

There are four stages of HE, and the first stage is a lack of awareness either in euphoria or anxiety, often with abnormal mood swings. Your sleep pattern also gets disturbed in the first stage; you can be awake all night, and sleep the whole day or at least be drowsy during the day and nap frequently. You fail to retain information like you used to before. The symptoms are so subtle they are easy to overlook. One example, I remember I kept getting calls from bill collectors to pay bills, which was really kind of strange.

I had enough money in my bank account to be able to pay my bills; I was working. Karl must have noticed me getting those calls and said to me one day, *"Are you paying your bills?"* I said, *"Well, no, I need to get around to it. But I keep forgetting about things that I need to do,"* he said, *"Would you like me to pay your bills for you?"* "Yes, that's probably a good idea," I said. I remember very vividly just saying, 'that's probably a good idea' because I kept on forgetting.

Forgetfulness is a basic feature of HE. It looks very much like procrastination, but it's not, because you do not put the task aside to do it later, you actually forget about it. It's like one moment you are like, 'Okay, I got this, have got to pay it.' You put it down on the table, and the next moment you forget about it completely: It's gone from your mind.

I was stressed and decided to come clean with Karl. I told him that I was in no way ready to plan the wedding or even think about it until I graduated. Graduating before diverting my attention to planning a wedding would compromise my Ph.D. This was not acceptable to me, nor was it to my mother. She had never expressed what she thought I should do, but she was so very proud of her daughter pursuing doctoral studies. She was beyond excited about completing my Ph.D., and if for any reason I did not, she would be tremendously disappointed. Karl was very perceptive about it, and we mutually agreed to postpone the wedding until my degree was complete.

Among all the chaos, I was pushing hard to make it through everything. HE is a neuropsychiatric syndrome, which occurs due to biochemical disturbance of brain function caused by liver failure. A healthy liver metabolizes all the nitrogenous substances of gut origin, including ammonia, mercaptan, and octopamine. However, in the case of liver failure, these substances are not metabolized. They get circulated by blood and cross the blood-brain barrier, which leads to HE.

With HE, the person not only is the person not aware, they are often irritable when confronted with lapses in basic responsibilities. I was not sleeping, which I did not know is also a characteristic of this condition – the reversal of the sleep/wake cycle.

My Dad, My Hero

Nearly every girl sees her dad as her hero. My dad was not only a hero but a true warrior and a survivor. He was my inspiration. He was very ill back then; even though his mind was very sharp, his body was shutting down. The problem that arose was kidney failure. First, he had a heart attack, and then they diagnosed COPD, Chronic Obstructive Pulmonary Disease, and now this kidney failure was yet another challenge for him.

I already talked about my father in chapter two. He lost both of his parents when he was in his mid-20s, and I believe this is one of the reasons my dad felt like he would have a shortened life span. I do not think he ever thought that he would live past 50. He was right; he did have a shortened lifespan. He died when he was only 71. Dad was an imposing man with charming looks, dark hair, and tall height. He faced a lot of health issues when he was younger. As I mentioned before, he had tuberculosis, and he had to stay in a sanitarium for two years. He was an example of how adversity would make you stronger. He had a strong will, and at the same time, he was very kind. He had a heart of gold, but he had an exterior of iron. He was very loyal and committed to his family. He could be very tough on us growing up. He wanted us to succeed. He wanted us to behave and grow up as good young adults, but to be honest, we were not always so well behaved.

Growing up, I recall him saying, *"I do not know how someone who sounds like an elephant going up and down the stairs can ice skate so gracefully."* I also recall coming downstairs to show off the skating costumes I made. After I spent hours and hours making my outfit, my mother showered me with compliments, and my father's comment was: *"You look like a pipe cleaner stuck out of a tent."* He was really quite a character. All our neighborhood friends loved my mother and were afraid of him.

I remember Karl and I spent a lot of time with my dad early in the summer of 1997. When he was recovering from coronary by-pass surgery that was the time he relied on oxygen. It was probably because they removed one of his lungs when he had tuberculosis, and he was a long term heavy smoker.

One of the things that were integral to my father's routine was his lunch with a group of friends. He was very committed to a group of people that he would lunch with once a week his whole life. He had not been able to go for several months because he was very ill and he was on oxygen. One day, Karl and I were both at my parents' home and said, "*I'd like to go to lunch.*" We were pleased to be able to fulfill his wish.

We got into the car and went to the restaurant where he met his friends for lunch. He said, "*I think I'm going to leave my oxygen in the car. Hey, Patty, you will come, get it if I need it, won't you?*" I said, "*Sure.*" Everybody was thrilled to see him after months. They all greeted him warmly, friends, and staff. We sat down at a table, a bit away from the rest of the people that he usually sat with. He just wanted to be careful to protect his energy.

One by one, all of these men came over and shook dad's hand. It was such a delight to witness; it felt like a scene straight out of The Godfather. It was as if they were honoring him, saying, "We thank you for coming out." I had not seen my father this happy in a long time. They all understood his condition and did not take much of his time. They just greeted him and left. I believe he needed this type of therapy; it held much importance to him.

As an occupational therapist, I strongly believe one of the most difficult parts of illness and disability is the interruption of usual routines. When those routines get disrupted, it really deprives a lot of meaning from one's life. This was true for my father, as his long-standing routines had a lot of meaning to him.

Dad ate about half of his lunch, and after a while, he said, *"Okay, I'm ready to go back,"* so we took him home. He was content and slept for the rest of the afternoon.

A few months later, I took my father for lunch at one of his favorite restaurants. We arrived, and he just looked at me and said, *"Patty, I cannot. I do not have the energy to go into the restaurant."* I said, *"How about I get you a takeaway meal?"* He said, *"That would be fine."* So, I got some food to take out and drove across the street to the ocean. It was a cold and somewhat rainy day, and we were one of relatively few cars. No one was on the beach, aside from a few low-tide joggers.

Dad had just lost his appetite and said to me, *"I just cannot eat, but it's nice to be out, and I appreciate it."* So, we sat there in the car for a long time. I was feeding French fries to the seagulls, and he was talking. He said, *"You know; if I had known that I was living this long, I would have taken much better care of myself."*

Then he started talking about my liver cirrhosis and failure. He said to me, *"You have to do what you have to do to survive. Take care of yourself, follow the medical advice. But do not let it interfere with the way you live."* He also told me that Karl is a good man, and he will take care of me. I just listened to him carefully. He said, *"But you have to take care of yourself."*

I remember this conversation vividly. My father was not a man to be introspective. It really meant a lot to me in terms of sharing that moment with him. I got to know a side of him I had rarely seen.

My father was very kind, and he loved his family. He further said, *"I would like to have been healthier to be a good grandfather. Unfortunately, I watch your mother, who is having so much fun with the grandkids, but I do not have the energy to get out of the chair and play with them. I wish I did."* I deeply felt every word that he spoke, and I have never felt so much respect and love towards my father. Even after all this, he was worried about my health and how he regretted not being able to play with his grandkids. It was just such a wonderful time, but I had to go back to Miami.

Hepatic Encephalopathy – Stage Two

The second stage of HE is marked by lethargy and major personality changes, including shortened attention span and forgetfulness. There is also minimal disorientation for time or place, followed by impulsive behavior and impaired ability to figure things out (like calculation of numbers) in your head.

In the spring of 1997, I was slowly moving into stage two of this lethal condition. However, I was still completely unaware. As I said before, one of the symptoms of this condition is a lack of insight by the person who has it.

Therefore, I did not know that I was altered, was having cognitive problems, and was not sleeping for a reason. You are mostly tired during the day and wide awake at night. It's interesting because the encephalopathy was affecting me in ways that I can only understand looking back today.

I was pretty sick at the time. My sister Michelle went up to spend time with my parents. I remember she was leaving our hometown. She called me, and I said, *"Michelle, ask mom if she needs help. Let me know because I can come up at any time."* Michelle told her, and I could hear my mother say in the background, *"Ask her how soon she can be here."* My mother would never say such a thing for no reason, and it was pretty alarming. I said to Michelle to tell her that I will be there as soon as I can.

I got off the phone and said to Karl, "I *have to go back*." He replied, "*I understand that you have to do what you have to do but be even more careful because you're not doing that well, either."* I was resistant.

It was the late summer of 1997.

I went back home, and my sister was still there. I remember it clearly because I drove to the grocery store with my nephew Brendan and something happened to me. As soon as I got out of the car and started walking, I felt very dizzy. I felt the need to sit down immediately, so I sat down on a high curb. I felt like I was going to pass out. I vomited blood in front of four-year-old Brendan, looked at him, and said, *"We're going home."*

I drove off home, not feeling very good about driving in that condition with a four-year-old in the car. When I got home, I just said, *"I'm sorry. I got to the store, and I did not feel well, so I came back without getting whatever it was that I was supposed to get."*

That was the beginning of the bleeding varices. Again, I was unaware. I was pretty confused, so I did not make any sense of it. Looking back now, I can clearly see that it was the beginning of late-stage liver failure.

It was getting worse over time. I remember one day, back in Miami, I was returning home from work, and after driving for a while, I found myself in a neighborhood that was not on my route. I thought to myself, how did I get here? I had no answer to the question. Though I knew where I was, it was a familiar place, but it just was not the place where I was supposed to be. That is what was happening. I would start driving and just forget where I was going. I would drive aimlessly, and it was a lack of awareness. I just was not thinking, which means I should not have been driving in the first place.

Things like this were becoming routine. Back in Miami, I would go to the grocery store, and as soon as I got inside, I would completely forget what I was supposed to buy. It was disorienting. I was moving into the third phase of HE because I was unaware of where I was going.

There's another interesting story my colleagues told me that happened at the university. They told me how I came into work one day. My long, dark, and curly hair flew all over the place, and my arms were full of paper. I said, *"Okay, I need the conference room for the next three hours,"* because I had that amount of time to get the final manuscript of my dissertation organized and send it over to the graduation office for approval so that I could graduate. As I said before, forgetfulness is seen as procrastination, but it's not. A week would go by, and you are like, *"Oh, I should have done this earlier,"* but I did get everything done. I did successfully defend my dissertation, and I did graduate in spring 1997, but it was tough for me to organize everything due to forgetfulness. Fortunately, I survived it.

I thank my determination to complete my dissertation and earn my Ph. D because that is the only thing that went right during that time. It kept me sane and gave me a short-term goal to focus on. I was driven to get it done. Giving up was not an option. I was not going to be ABD (All But Dissertation). There are a lot of people who are ABD. They have finished everything except their dissertation and would just give up on it because it's lengthy, time-consuming, and requires perseverance. However, I was not going to be one of them, and I proved that to myself.

That summer of 1997, I was teaching a class, and that is when I became aware that something was really wrong with me. I was all over the place, forgetting things, and getting sleepy between the lectures. I was forgetful and which was very unlike me. I was acting strange and realized that I was not myself at all. At that point, the third stage of HE had set in.

Hepatic Encephalopathy – Stage Three

The third stage is confusion at its worst. You are unable to figure out what's going on around you, and reality makes zero sense to you. You have an intense desire to sleep, but you still are aware of the world around you, and you are respondent to verbal stimuli. You lose your sense of direction very badly. This last statement about direction and confusion can also relate to household appliances.

One day, Karl approached me: *"Patty, why is there an iron in the refrigerator?"* I responded... *"an iron in the refrigerator?"* He asked me to come with him. He opened the refrigerator. There was the iron, among the lettuce, mustard, and peaches.

Hmmm, I don't really know. And started giggling, *"But I am sure there was a good reason..."*

The telltale ironing board was in the room as well. *"Did you get anything ironed?"* he asked? And we both laughed. Clearly, I was the one who put the iron in the refrigerator. Did I have any memory of it? NO.

The stories of what happens while someone had Stage 3 Encephalopathy are often hilarious – upon reflection. Not so much when they are happening.

Cirrhosis and its side effects

Cirrhosis is the medical term for scarring of the liver. A number of processes can cause it. Some causes for cirrhosis are autoimmune hepatitis, infectious hepatitis, alcohol use, and fatty liver disease. Cirrhosis results in experiences of weakness, loss of appetite, easy bruising, yellowing of the skin and eyes (what we call jaundice), itching, and fatigue.

When you get to a point where your liver is hugely scarred with cirrhosis, two things can happen, one of them is called ascites. It is swelling of the abdomen, hips, thighs, legs, ankle, and foot. It happens because your liver cannot absorb the fluid in your body, and it gets absorbed into the tissues instead. As a result, you get considerable weight gain due to fluid accumulation.

Moreover, there are enlarged veins in the esophagus called esophageal varices. In this condition, the veins in your lower esophagus become swollen because the blood flow to the liver is backed up. They eventually can leak blood and rupture, which causes severe internal bleeding, which could be life-threatening.

Hepatic Encephalopathy – Stage Four

Then comes the fourth stage, the most critical of all; coma. It is a condition in which the person is unable to respond to verbal or non-verbal stimuli. If a coma is not treated well, in time, it can result in death. Forty-one percent of patients who go into a coma actually end up losing their lives. That is why it is essential to keep this condition under control.

I was worried, but I did not lose hope. I was spending a fair amount of time going back and forth to my gastroenterologist and was following every guideline very carefully at that point. Even the Prednisone was just not helping me. That is when they knew that this is the time, and I was referred to the transplant team.

The Final Destination – A Liver Transplant

Trust me, once we accepted the need for a liver transplant, it became a lot easier, and we just went on with our lives. We did not have much choice. We just had to deal with it if that is what was written for me and was going to happen. You have to do what you have to do, therefore, is the basis of this chapter.

Waiting for the transplant can be torturous. They take it very slowly, ensuring you are a good candidate and that you are healthy enough to survive a complicated surgery and recovery. I was ready to start and determined to get involved with the transplant team at Jackson Memorial Hospital in Miami. By that point, it was pretty clear we would not be able to schedule the wedding anytime soon.

When Things Fell Apart...

It took me a while to learn this lesson, but it holds immense importance to me. When things are falling apart, pay attention, and try to maintain yourself together. Especially when it comes down to your physical health, do not become a victim. I learned from my dad to try to stay strong and healthy because, at the end of the day, *you have to do what you have to do!*

During that summer, I found myself increasingly fatigued and became more forgetful over time. My joints ached, and even though I was sick, I went running four times a week. I never wanted to be sick in the first place. When I went into liver failure, I never slowed down, never stopped. I was heading into work every day. I completed my dissertation. I was there for my family whenever they needed me because I was not giving up, and I had tied myself to what my father had told me.

When the time came for my liver transplant, I started questioning myself. Should I have stopped working? Should I have stopped living my life and fulfilling my responsibilities? I knew the answer was no. Definitely not. This is not who I was and how I was brought up to be. I never fell into the trap of going on disability leave, and then having to sit around and wait for my will to motivate me. I stood strong against my condition, just like my father, and never gave up on my will to live. I did everything that I had to.

"Empaths did not come into this world to be victims; we came to be warriors. Be brave. Stay strong. We need all hands on deck."

-Anthon St. Maarten

Chapter 6
Farewell

The Hardest Goodbye

I cannot imagine growing up without my father. My father, although rough and tough, supported my dreams and celebrated my successes. For me, he is that strong pillar that never falters and withstands all sorts of hurricanes and storms, both for himself and me. My father was my hero, despite his faults. My father, too, taught me things that will stay with me for a lifetime. I wanted him to stay with me forever, and never in my worst nightmares did I imagine losing him, but unfortunately, I did.

The fall of 1997 is fresh as a daisy in my mind. Everything happened swiftly. Something I gravely feared was about to happen, I could sense it in the air. During my trip to my hometown in Massachusetts, my father and I talked about the diseases he was suffering from while he was still in the hospital. The kidney failure was slowly sucking the life out of him. He told me that he and my mother together made a decision. At that time, the only thing keeping him alive was his dialysis trips twice a week. He was bedridden in a Skilled Nursing Facility. They had talked to the priest, who was very important. My father was not a religious man. However, he had tremendous respect for my mother's faith. They decided that when the time was right, my father would leave the hospital and come home on hospice care. However, my father said that he did not want to do it soon because he wished not to ruin his brother Dick and sister in law Sondra's 70th birthday parties. He said he would wait until the time was right.

Dad was in the middle of kidney failure, and the doctors said that if he decided to go home, he would only have 72 hours to live. Essentially, the fluid in his system was, without treatment, would rise to a fatal level. The doctor told him that it is not going to be a very painful but peaceful death.

It was already very difficult for me to digest my father's illness, but what came next was the biggest challenge. He had asked me to only keep this plan to myself. He said, "*I am telling you, but I'm not telling your brothers and sisters. I really do not want to create a lot of fuss about this. So, I would be happy if you could respect the fact that I really do not want anyone to know.*"

I had no choice but to respect dad's decision. I decided to keep this to myself until my father was ready to tell everyone. It's just one of those decisions that I came to regret afterward. He had asked me, and I respected his right to make his own choice.

I also felt bad because my brothers and sisters should have had the same right as I did over the information about our father making this huge decision. So it was one of those really tough decisions, but I did not have much time to worry about it. I went back to Miami, and two weeks later, I got a phone call that he was home on hospice.

I started panicking. I did not know what to do and was very upset. I called Dr. Barkin and said, *"This is what I need to do; I need to go home because my father is home on hospice. I know that I am sick, but I have to do it. What recommendations do you have?"*

He wanted me to take an Ativan or a similar antianxiety medication. He said, *"I know you will not take it, but I would really like it if you do."* I said, *"No, I do not want to take that."* I did what I had to and went home on Friday.

It was September 13th, 1997. I got home just in time to see my father, still awake enough to recognize me. He said, *"Patty, I hope you understand that I had to do this."*

He decided the time was right when my older sister Joanne came to visit. Joanne is strong and has always been the person in the family you can count on. It took a strong will for him even to let us know, and Joanne could handle it. He wanted one of his daughter's home to support my mother and to be beside him through all of this. It was a good decision

> *"To a father growing old, nothing is dearer than a daughter."*
>
> ### *-Euripides*

The time to bid farewell to my father had finally come. It was the moment that was not awaited, the moment I dreaded the most. I was not ready to face all of this at all, but I had to. I was constantly on the phone with Dr. Barkin telling him my condition. My dad passed away that night. I was up all night; I could not sleep and be just too upset even to shut my eyes. I could not help but think about everything dad told me when I took him out for lunch the last time. Everything was coming back like a flashback, and my heart was aching.

Starting the next day, my memories became confused and chaotic. Our other sister Michelle was coming home to Massachusetts. She learned of my father's death as she was leaving her home in Hilton Head SC. I got on the phone and arranged flights for Karl, my brothers, and Michelle's boys.

Michelle's two boys were young, six, and eight at that time. I got them on a plane from Hilton Head, South Carolina, to Charlotte. I got Karl on a plane from Miami to Charlotte. My brother, Fred, was also on his way; he had a flight from Orlando, Florida, to Charlotte. Karl was running around, picking up everyone arriving at the Charlotte airport. All four of them were on the plane to Charlotte from Boston. Karl made it all work.

I was eagerly waiting for them all to arrive. However, by the time they arrived the next day, I was actually in ICU in a coma.

The Horrible Decision

That morning, on Saturday, we were dealing with the arrangements. On the same day, the mail came, and it made me so sad. Inside it was a card that my cousin Stacie's children, Zack and Kedian, had made. It said, *"Uncle Jack, get healthy soon. We are rooting for you."* Poor kids did not know that his uncle had died the night before. It came the day after he passed away and my sisters, mother and I just sobbed when we saw it.

The day was getting tougher with every passing second. Since I did not get much sleep, I had a really bad headache. That night with the headache, I could not sleep again. I moved around in my parent's medicine cabinet, looking for something that might help. Finally, I took Advil. I could sense that something was wrong with me. By 7:00 AM, I was throwing up blood. My mother came downstairs, and I was in the bathroom, throwing up blood right after she just lost her husband. This made me feel embarrassed and bad.

Mom found me and went like, "Oh Patricia! What happened to you?" and I just kept throwing up blood. She said, *"Should I call an ambulance, or should I take you to the hospital?"* I said, *"Mom, the last thing you need right now is an ambulance at the house, right after dad died. If you do not mind, you could just take me to the hospital and drop me off and come back home. You do not even have to come in."*

The Enameled Pan

A really interesting thing happened that morning, which shocked me quite a lot. Mom brought down to me this enameled pan that we always used as a spit-up pan when we were kids. *"Here! You are going to need this in the car."* I thought, *I do not want blood in this pan.* I took some plastic grocery bags and put them in the pan. Just the idea of that particular pan she took to the hospital with me has stuck with me for a long time. It was something unusual and completely unexpected, especially when you have so many memories related to it.

Anyway, mom and I pulled up in front of the emergency room, and I said, *"Mom, just let me go in,"* and she said, *"No, I'm going to get somebody to take you in. Sit right there."*

Out Of My Mind

Of course, I was not in the right mindset because I had just lost my father, and I was encephalopathic. I had a plastic bag full of blood in my hand. I do not know what came into my head. I took that plastic bag and threw it in the trash can, which you are not supposed to do. You are not supposed to throw blood in a trash can, but I was just not in my right mind, and I did not want anyone to feel gross doing it for me. I, therefore, decided to do it myself.

The hospital immediately rushed me to the emergency room. My mother called her doctor, who happened to be in the hospital. I remember very vividly that I kept trying to find my insurance card and driver's license, but I could not. Mom said, *"Can I help you?"* and I agreed. I handed her my wallet, and she came up with them right away. That's when I realized how confused I was.

They took me into the emergency room. I was on a stretcher by that time. To determine the criticality of the situation, they asked me questions like what color was the blood? Was it dark, or was it bright red, and in an instance, I just threw up again right there in the emergency room. I had sent my mother home, but I do not think she went.

The doctor kept asking me to tell him exactly what was going on with me, and it kind of came to me backward, echoing. The next thing I remember is that I was in the Intensive Care Unit, and it was a couple of days later that I even realized where I was. It is horrible not knowing where you are and what exactly happened that led you to be in a hospital bed. It can leave you confused and frustrated, and that's exactly what happened.

I was unable to make sense out of anything for days. I did not know anything about my father's burial and the family's situation. I was just lying on the bed.

I believe my sisters called Karl and told him what was going on with me before he got on the plane. I was in the hospital by 8 AM, and his plane was to arrive by noon. As soon as he arrived, there was a family lunch, then my sisters brought him to the hospital.

Since my condition was critical, they were just not letting anyone come in. The hospital staff asked Karl if he was a family member, and he started to think of things to say when my older sister said, *"Yes, he's a family member."* That's when it hit him and made him realize what it is like not having official status. He knew that it was going to be a problem for him in a situation where my family was not there. It turned out to be kind of a wakeup call.

The Funeral

I had missed my father's funeral, which was about three days after his death. It made me so sad to even think about it, but I was helpless. One thing that I do remember is trying to talk the nurses into having an ambulance drive me to the church so I could just be there while the funeral happened. I said I would stay in the back of the church, and no one would know that I was there. I could do the service, and then they could take me back to the hospital before anyone got out of the service.

Of course, I knew I got nowhere with that conversation. I did try, despite being unaware of what I was asking. I wanted to be with my family in such a difficult time. Unfortunately, there was something else written in my fate. The HE coma in Stage 4 is the biggest problem that you face when the late symptoms of hepatic encephalopathy show up. You do not realize or understand anything.

Cognitive Testing

I remember while I was in the hospital, a doctor came in to do a mini-mental status exam. The doctor asked me, *"Who is the current president?"* The president was Bill Clinton at that time, and I knew it, but strangely, I could not come up with his name. Then he asked me what year it was and I could not answer it either. Then he asked me, *"Do you know where you are?"* and I said, *"Yes, in a hospital."* He said, *"Okay, which hospital?"* I said, *"I do not know."* He then asked me how old I was, *"I am 29,"* then he told me to rest and left.

The next morning, he came back, and before he could ask me, I said, *"Bill Clinton is the president, wife Hillary, and daughter Chelsea, I am at South Shore Hospital in Weymouth, Massachusetts, and I am 44 years old."* To which he said, *"Well, obviously, you're much better."*

During that time, my brothers, my cousins, and Karl came to see me, and I do not remember any of them visiting until the last day when Karl and John came to see me. I saw them quickly, and then they had to leave because they had their return flights. Karl had to fly back with the boys, Scott and Brendan, so he could not stay with me. Michelle's boys, still could not understand why they were not allowed to see me. This was because children were not allowed in the ICU, and the kids were pretty upset about it.

Although I have little memory of the situation, my sister Michelle has filled me in on the details. Apparently, I was very demanding, unaware of the severity of my situation, and insisted on going to my father's funeral to the point where I had to be restrained. She reports I did not recognize anyone or anything. It is embarrassing to think I acted that way, but I realize I cannot feel bad, as I have no responsibility for situations under which I was not in voluntary control. And, this was one of them. There were many more to come.

The Side Effects

I was learning new and interesting facts about hepatic encephalopathy. It is a neurotoxic disorder. In my role as an occupational therapy professor, I knew this was not one of the terms generally covered. Although I do not teach Neuroscience, I was always explaining to students about medical terms and neurological disorders. HE was not one of them. Not only will it be in the future, but this was when I found out for real what it means.

I also experienced apraxia. One day when I was in the hospital, I was trying to call my parents' home. I have always known the number is 749-2929. When I asked them, they gave me a portable phone because they did not have telephones in ICU. I was trying to dial the number, which I clearly still remember, but I could not go past a few digits at a time. I was dialing seven then, I have to talk myself through 7-4, and I would push the 4; then 7-4-9 and I would push the 9; I would never get to push the 2 as, by that time, the call had timed out. The phone has a certain time limit to dial the number, and I was taking too long. I was going crazy because I could not even dial a number on my own. When I could not dial it after multiple tries, I had to have the nurses actually make the phone call for me, and it was frustrating to the core.

Another thing that I have mentioned previously is the reversed sleep cycle. I remember one night in particular. I was just lying on my bed, watching the clock strike one o'clock and then two o'clock. Frustratingly, I pressed the button to call the nurse and said, *"I cannot take this anymore; it's awful."*

I remember this nurse very vividly. She was tall, with very short bleached white hair with a long skinny braid in the back. She was so upset with me. She said, *"Listen, just go to sleep."* I said, *"I cannot! That's why I keep calling you; I cannot go to sleep."* She said, *"You have encephalopathy. You're toxic. We cannot give you anything to make you fall asleep. We're trying to clear everything out of you."* She would stay for a few minutes and then leave, but I called her again and again.

They ended up moving me closer to the nurses' station, where they could watch over me. They saw it as the only option of putting things right. Something that I found out when I read my medical records was that I was an annoying patient. I was scared; I felt that either I was at some battle that they wanted to put me closer, or just to avoid the hassle it took for them to attend to me whenever I called from way down the hall.

I also remember the man in the next room. This man would just keep coughing and moaning. He kept calling out the nurses that he was dying. It was awful to listen to. I seem to remember I felt so bad that I wanted to talk to him, but of course, I could not get out of bed. It was a really confusing and frustrating time, and I have frightening memories of that hospitalization.

Finally, they put me in a room on a general medical floor, and I had a new roommate once again. I had long and curly hair at that time that was matted. One day I was sitting in a chair, trying to get knots out of my hair. The woman, who was in the next bed, was constantly trying to talk to me. I tried to talk to her, but I was unable. I was aphasic, and the words would not come out of my mouth the way I formulated them in my brain. The things I said to her did not have anything to do with what I'm trying to say. It was complete nonsense. In those ways, I could now provide my students with real-life examples of aphasia, apraxia, and encephalopathic coma.

So, back to the story, I just apologized to the woman in the next bed, and she said, *"I do things like that all the time."* It was all so frustrating, but I did get better. My recovery was slow, but the day I got out of the hospital, I felt so much better.

I was in the hospital for five days, to be exact. I remember my mother and my sister came to pick me up. On our way home, my sister said, *"We're going to stop by dad's grave."*

I was not ready for that, but looking back now, it felt good. It was helpful as I had lost that important time. My memory had skipped a few critical days, and I was just like, *"Whoa, what happened?"* The other thing that they did was they had videos made of the funeral for me. It was really strange watching those because I was still not in quite the right mind. Nonetheless, I watched them, I appreciated their effort, and my mom deleted them later.

That's when it all came back to me, and I vividly remembered what had happened. It was the toughest period of my life, but I had even tougher things to deal with. I came out stronger of every battle, and with the support of my family, I was able to get over everything life had put me through. Though nothing can ever fulfill the emptiness that you feel when you lose a parent, you must accept the reality. My dad was my hero, and he will always be right here inside my heart.

"A father holds his daughter's hand for a short while, but he holds her heart forever."

-Unknown

Part II
Crisis Years 1998-2007

Chapter 7
The Toxins and the First Transplant

After everything that happened, my body was getting weaker. Each passing day was getting difficult to get through. The hepatologist who was taking care of me in Massachusetts, until I returned to Miami warned me that I would have to go back and get a transplant right away. Clearly, I still had not fully processed the extent of my liver failure and the urgency of my situation. *"They do not really do that to people,"* meaning replace livers, and my doctor said, *"If you want to live to be a little old lady, you are going to have to get a transplant."* And I frustratingly said, *"No."*

Soon, I was back in Miami to prepare for my first liver transplant. As soon as I got back, they put me into the transplant evaluation program, the one I could not get into before I left. However, I guess bleeding varices and a hepatic coma qualifies you quickly.

The Transplant Support Group

Karl and I decided that we will take every possible opportunity to prepare ourselves before going for a transplant. There came a time when Karl and I decided to attend the pre-transplant support group sessions. It was an interesting time. A pre-transplant support group is a group of people who get together at least once a month and talk about how their journey is, their medical history, condition/disease mandating a transplant, and the list goes on. There was also a group of people who had been around for a while. They were living with a transplant. We found out a lot about what exactly happens during and after the transplant. I clearly remember how it was so very helpful to go to that group.

The doctors had just recently told me that it could be hard to get an organ because I was a small adult, and I would be in the same group as adolescents with my size. They can not put a liver inside a body if it's too big. A smaller liver will grow to fit. A large one simply was not going to work for me. That said, there were a lot of people in that group waiting for a transplant. Moreover, B positive is a rare blood type. I needed a B positive donor and only about 17% of the population is B positive.

You cannot donate blood if you are waiting for a transplant. I appreciate people who just donate blood I thank them for doing so, as I would not have made it through my surgeries without transfusions. I only wish I could give back. It is a tradition in my family to donate blood regularly, and I am sorry I am not in the group.

Awareness is Crucial

One thing I learned at the transplant support group is that it's important to talk to your family about your wishes about donation actively. It is not just about being an organ donor by having it on your license. You have to be responsible enough to let your family know. Even though you're an organ donor, if something happens to you and you pass away, it's no longer your decision. You must have that conversation: In any emergency, medical personnel will try to reach the family and then decide. You need to inform your siblings, parents, and friends your feelings about organ donation. Suppose they know what you choose to do. It will help them make difficult decisions.

Once I talked to one of my very good friends, and she said, *"I'm not a donor."* I said, *"Really, why?"* She said, "*I think it's my body, my decision, and I just do not want anyone carrying around my organs. That is too creepy."* I responded, saying, *"Think about two things that you think you are going to lose by donating that? Is there anything? I guess not. It's not something that you lose; it's something you are going to get. You get the satisfaction of being able to save someone's life!"*

The Pre-Transplant

Back in Miami, I was at a hospital going through pre-transplant. It was six weeks before I completed all the testing and evaluations. I was so relieved I qualified for the transplant list. During that time, I was probably in and out of the hospital due to encephalopathy about three times.

Before the transplant, it was important to stop the bleeding varices. They would put something like a rubber band around varices, so they stopped bleeding. This procedure is also called Esophageal Banding or ligation. They also have to replace the rubber bands about once a month, so it was not much fun to have this problem.

A Source of Support

My brother John and I would have long telephone conversations during this time. He was dealing with his own life challenges, and his introspection and empathy were most welcomed. John is a thoughtful listener, rare in our family growing up, as we continually interrupt each other with our thoughts. I loved these conversations. John is also a poet, while he is not building houses or restoring his prized sailboat Trade winds. I have included a couple of his poems in this book. One is at the beginning of Chapter 4, and another is here.

Conversations with my brother reminded me that support could come from someone who lives far away. A friend, or family member, even when far away, can be a great emotional support. John wrote this one for me about having trouble sleeping.

Who besides the Owl

It is late
In the night
I have pain
Cannot sleep
Are there others
this world

Share the schedule
I keep

Thinking on that
As my mind
Takes to
Wonder

There are
Surely a lot
I surmise
yes I ponder

If any
Gain ground
What pressure They're under

This continuous
Pain
Not just passing
Like thunder

In a wonderful book
I read
How some
Overcame cancer

Amazement of
all how
Their mind
Found an answer

In still
others I read
of potential
Within

And that fear
Only fear
Blocks the
Path to begin
                              -John Charles Scott Jr

My First Liver Transplant

When they called that they had a liver ready for me, I had mixed feelings of happiness and nervousness. I went to the hospital with Karl and two of our friends, Michelle, who is a nurse, and John, both good friends. They were both with us to support and lightened the tension that built up in the air. I guess that helped.

I went to the surgical ICU afterward. I adjusted to the surgical ICU very quickly because everything went very smoothly for this first transplant. I was probably discharged to the transplant recovery floor in a day.

My transplant surgery was the first surgery I ever had. In fact, my only prior hospitalizations were that fall, the September 1997 episode for the encephalopathic coma, and then rehospitalizations for the encephalopathy and banding. So, February 28th of 1998 was my first surgery. I had never experienced this kind of pain before. Upon transfer, I was noticing the absence of the nurses to give me something for the pain to which I apparently said, "Well, I feel that nurses should be taking care of me... I am in pain." A medical assistant responded, "They have to report on other patients as the shift changed." Then to Michelle, who was with me, I said, "I think it's time to get out of here."

To be honest, I was not myself. I am not like that normally. Michelle recounted the story to me later. I believe it was an after-effect of coming out of the ICU. The nurses are hovering over you all the time. Later, I said, "What's wrong with these nurses, where are they?" "I'm scared." I was indeed scared as well as in pain. The medical assistant told me later that she thought... *they were going to have their hands full with this patient.*

She turned out to be one of my favorite medical assistants. She had this idea of me, and for good reason, until later, when she realized that I was civilized and under control. They realized I was okay, and they really began liking me. Good thing as I was to be what they call a "frequent flier."

The After Effects

When I did go home after my first transplant, it was very hard for me to keep up with my bloodwork done at least twice a week. I was really tired, and any movement hurt terribly. Riding in a car was torture. It was a lot of hassle for me to go, wait for my name to be called, give the blood sample to the vampires, and then wait to see the doctor and get the results. At first, Karl would stay with me, and then, after a while, when I was stronger, he would drop me at the clinic, go home, and then come pick me up again. Doing this twice a week was no less than torture.

I remember there was a woman who had a transplant at the same time that I did. She was back to work after two weeks, and I cannot imagine how she did that. The other thing she did was taking the metro rail (public transportation in Miami) because she did not have a car. I was going crazy thinking about how she can do that. There I was complaining about walking in and walking out of the house, getting into the car, walking through the front door up to the elevator, and going to the third floor to get myself checked. My body was still not allowing me to do the hard work. Then there was this woman. I could not believe it, but she did so well!

Anyway, I got a bit better with time but only for three months.

At three months, they did my bloodwork, it was not good, so they did some tests, and I had what they called hepatic artery stenosis which is a side effect that you do not want to have. This was my first realization that if there were a rare side effect, which maybe 5% of patients, or even less, I would experience it, and then I will be one of the small numbers of people who get it. Lucky me. Since Hepatic Artery Stenosis deprives the liver of much-needed oxygen, the tissue in my newly transplanted liver would eventually die. Clearly, NOT a good situation.

So, in April of 1998, I immediately had another surgery to replace the damaged artery with a healthy one from my groin. It was unsuccessful. There were several more surgeries to find a solution to drain my bile – all to no avail. It seemed to work for about three hours, and then it stopped. I was in that situation for probably three weeks. Meanwhile, they were trying to find another liver for me. Soon, I caught my own personal Roto-Rooter system.

Chapter 8
When the best things happen amongst the crisis

The Realization

In life, we all go through moments where we believe that it cannot get worse. Hope is elusive, and it appears the darkness is going to stay for a long time, and we may wonder if we will ever see the light again. Likewise, when we fall sick, we often lose sight of the good. This is what it is like being in and out of the hospital. What we forget among all of the chaos is that the world has a way of finding the light. I had found Karl, and he proved to be my right hand and greatest strength.

Karl not only gave me strength but also the will to live. He supported me to be the best self I could desire, and, I will say, need to continue with my work. He knew how important my students were to me. Karl made everything possible. I came home from work each day, exhausted and ready for bed. He was there, with a beautiful dinner ready, he encouraged me to do what I needed to do to take care of myself, and he handled the rest. I wanted to heal because I saw so much life in Karl, and his love for me was a compelling reason to get the physical strength back to be a true co-equal partner. I wanted to live with him the life I always dreamed of. He was always there for me and stood strong with me through thick and thin. Had it not been for Karl, if he was not with me during that time, I am not sure if I would have made it.

At this point, I want to step back to September. A lot happened during the time I was at the hospital during my father's funeral. Since we were not officially married, Karl faced many difficulties, sometimes with the procedures and other times the queries he had to go through just to meet his fiancé. He realized that he was too old to be just my boyfriend. He knew that he will face limitations and will have no right to see me whenever he wanted to. This way, he could not really help me out.

At this point, Karl and I had been engaged for eight months. So when he returned to Hingham to bring me back to Florida, he sat beside me, and said, *"I know it is really bad timing, but we have to get married before this transplant."* He never failed to surprise me and make the happiest at the same time. It was the last thing on my mind during those days.

The Arrangements

Although it surely was bad timing, it was the right thing to do

We were in Miami at the time, and Karl said to me, *"The only thing you have to do is get a dress for yourself and leave the rest to me. I'll take care of everything."* We mutually decided not to make a big fuss out of it and opt for a simple and happy wedding with just the two of us. However, you have to have witnesses to the wedding. So, in the plan, there were just four of us. It then got a little bit out of control, and in the end, there were ten people present at the wedding.

He did take care of everything, and our small wedding ceremony turned out to be the best thing that happened during the crisis.

Karl had a friend from his days at the United Nations, Helmut Horn. Helmut managed a group of hotels out of Chicago, and the Cheeca Lodge was one of his properties. Karl asked Helmut's help in making arrangements for our wedding, and he did in a heartbeat. He worked with the managers of the hotel and made all the arrangements.

The Craziest Wedding

Though we were in the middle of a crisis, it was a special day for both of us. Karl made sure to make it a day that I would remember forever. We wanted to get married on the pier at sunset, and so we did. I cannot describe in words just how beautiful and breathtaking it was. Ten of our friends were there. We had a suite at the Cheeca Lodge. The Cheeca Lodge is in Islamorada, Florida, about halfway from Miami to Key West. It was best known as the place George H.W. Bush would go bonefishing on the flats. His suite was right above ours. He, of course, was not there.

Two of my girlfriends, Sue and Michelle, came down with me the night before. I could not have been happier. The setup in our suite was beautiful. Everything was in perfect rhythm. There was a breathtaking view of the ocean. There was a beautiful spread of stone crabs with a variety of food, cheese, and crackers, and then there were several bottles of champagne. My friends looked at me, and I was like, *"GO FOR IT! I'm not drinking, but it does not mean you are not!"*

They had champagne. I enjoyed the excitement, the chaos, preparations, arrangements, and watching as we were getting ready for the wedding. Everything felt like a living and breathing dream. I will never forget Michelle's hilarious rendition of "Get Me to the Church on time." She invented the words, and we sang it over and over. I was so happy. Just a few days before I was in a hospital bed, I was now standing among precious friends, ready to get married to the love of my life.

I had shared with Karl a few things, and he made sure everything was well taken care of. The concierge made arrangements for the flowers, and took care of everything else, while Karl and I got ready for our big day. It was a beautiful wedding. The wedding was at sunset on the pier of Cheeca Lodge. The weather could not have cooperated better.

They had a small dining room that was overlooking the ocean, and that is where we had the reception since there were only 10 of us. We just let people order off the menu rather than coming up with a special menu of our own choice.

We also had a beautiful wedding cake, and there were champagne and wine to celebrate this day to the fullest. I had my own supply of sparkling water. We got the whole wedding experience, and it was the craziest wedding anyone would have ever attended.

I could not help but fall for Karl all over again. I mean, how amazing is a person who wants to marry a woman is on the transplant list? It was a beautiful night. When we took our vows, it was not just a narrative to us. Although I think when Karl said the words *"in sickness and in health,"* he did not quite know what he was getting himself into. After the ceremony and the dinner, we went up to the room, and there were about five or six people with us when Karl decided he was going to pick me up and carry me over the threshold of the hotel room. It was a very bad idea. I mean, come on! We were not fourteen, but forty, and somethings are not wise.

Anyway, he picked me up, got me over the threshold, and then he doubled over in pain. He put me down carefully. Thankfully, he did not drop me. He almost crawled into the bedroom. It was all fine in the end, but it sure made a different type of marriage night for us.

We settled in; fortunately, we had a suite with French doors open to the living room. Karl laid on the bed while the rest of us sat in the living room area for a while to have some fun. Later, Karl and I spent the night talking about things and discussing how our life is going to be.

The next morning, when we arrived at the restaurant for breakfast, we were greeted with applause. We did not realize the other guests had been watching the wedding the night before and knew we were the newly wedded couple. It never occurred to me that the restaurant's dining room was overlooking the pier where we got married. It was the most cheerful morning of my life.

Back to Routine

We had breakfast with our friends at the restaurant the morning after our wedding. After everything was done, everyone went their own way. Karl and I stayed another day; we decided to give ourselves a treat. One of the places we sought out was a hot tub that Karl needed badly after attempting to carry me over the threshold the night before.

As soon as we got home, Karl went to his chiropractor. He said, *"You know, my office in the Keys is about a mile from where you were. You know, you should have called me while you were in the hotel."* And Karl was like, *"Oh, well! It was my wedding, and I did not include many people."* And *they both laughed.* Anyway, that worked out fine.

Little did we know we were to witness our first ordeal as a couple soon after.

It was going to get pretty scary, but I did not worry anymore because I had Karl with me, my biggest support system. He showed his strength in the worst times, and how to never quit on people and situations. Our wedding was the only sane thing that happened amid all the chaos and everything going on in my life. I was so grateful that Karl asked me to get married before the transplant because I would have never survived without his support and genuine care. He sure came into my life like a miracle and gave me the power to overcome the things I thought were impossible for me to bear. That is why I always say, never be ungrateful. No matter what happens, stay strong, and find the people around you who are positive and constructive forces in your life. Avoid those who dwell on the negative, or the what if's.

"Difficult things take a long time, impossible things a little longer.

Chapter 9
The Hospitalizations
Seemed Never to Stop

"No one is so brave that he is not disturbed by something unexpected."

-Julius Caesar

Life is unpredictable. No one knows what is going to happen next, so we have a choice. We can wait in dread expecting the worse, OR we can proceed with our lives as though the sun will always shine more brightly every day. In my experience, I prefer to live anticipating the best. Anticipating the best will not protect you from the inevitable whenever it comes.

The unexpected will not always happen for the better; it sure turned my life upside down. In a blink of an eye, everything became a mess. You can never tell that you are going to turn from being an average healthy person at some point in life, seemingly in control, into a helpless, vulnerable person; I certainly did not know.

Following my first transplant, I went home, not knowing I was headed for re-hospitalization due to multiple reasons, and not just once but several times. The problem started in April 1998, six weeks after my first transplant.

Accepting the Inevitable

After I found out that I had hepatic artery stenosis, I had a second surgery, as I described before, which was unsuccessful. They put tubes through the skin into my liver once a month to drain an obstructed bile duct. The liver produces bile, which aids the digestion of fats. To open up the bile duct, they put a balloon in me. This whole process is called Percutaneous Transhepatic biliary drainage. They did that for a few years until my artery stayed open.

As a result, between 1998 and 2001, I was regularly visiting the hospital once a month for dilation of the bile duct to keep it open. After three years of going into the hospital for my never-ending roto-rooter treatment, sometimes staying overnight, other times longer depending on my infections, both bacterial and fungal, I finally had my bile duct repaired.

The time you spend in the hospital can be strange and depressing. After so many hospitalizations, Karl and I were never sure when the next shoe would drop, and I would be back in. For me, I would have no idea whether I was going to get out healthier or in an even worse condition. Many times anxiety takes over, but you have to take control of yourself, especially your mind. Do not let it wander. It is normal to have fearful thoughts, but it is also essential that you not let them take space in your head.

Every experience has its lessons, and those lessons can vary from person to person. I have learned through my experience that no matter how independent a human you are, or how much you hate letting others do things for you when you are sick and in a critical condition, you need to be dependent. Like it or not, and I never did; you are dependent. You have to listen to the instructions of health professionals. You must do what the nurses or the doctors are telling you to, without an argument. At that point, you just need to allow yourself to be taken care of. At times like this, I would tend to become irritable and demanding, hopefully not unreasonably, and the staff understood my situation. They knew at the time; I was not clear-minded, and my irritation was more of my frustration with the situation than with them. I was so sick that I was unable to make sense out of things.

Going back to work

After my first transplant, due to the complications, I was off from work for six months. I went back to work part-time in August 1998, and I was back full-time in January of 1999. During that time, I was still dealing with a lot of tenderness in my belly caused by monthly roto-rooter treatments and external bile drain. I used to wear lightweight and loose dresses, which did not put pressure on my belly. I had one such outfit, a dress: blue cotton corduroy overall except in a dress, no pants. Similar to overalls, it is low slung on the sides. One day I was giving a lecture and all of a sudden, everybody got quiet. I could not figure out what was going on, so I continued with my lecture. A few minutes later, after being asked a question, when I looked down casually, my heart skipped a beat. I saw that I had this colossal stain of bile on my white shirt. I looked at my students and said, *"Why did not you tell me. I could've done something about this,"* and they said, *"Well, we did not want you to get embarrassed."* I said, as confidently as I could, *"I'm not embarrassed, but I would have liked to stop the leak."*

It turned out to be a teachable moment, yet unfortunately, it was not an isolated incident. I had to deal with such things during that period, and it became quite normal for me. The key is to have a sense of humor because you have no other choice. The reason why I am saying this is your attitude towards things matter. Everything depends on how you deal with it. You have to wake up every day and remind yourself that *Hey! You are alive though your bile drain backed up overnight, and there is bile all over your bedding.*

The problem with the bile duct tubes and constant balloon dilatation procedures is that I had repetitive infections. At one point, I had to have a central line inserted because I needed to get powerful antibiotics.

When to stop the Roto-Rooter?

In June 2001, I recall we were sitting down with Dr. Tzakis, the Head of Transplantation, and my main man. Karl and I were getting an update on my condition. This was shortly after the stroke I had due to the misplacement of a central line by a surgical fellow. I needed to administer a powerful antibiotic for another infection. For clarification, he was a qualified general surgeon and was training to qualify as a transplant surgeon. He was very much qualified to insert the central line, but he just made a mistake, a big one.

So I asked Dr. Tzakis, *"When do we stop the 'Roto-Rooter' of my bile duct?"* Yeah, that's what I called it, roto-rooter. He said, *"Well. It's hard to say; we do not know if the duct is that well to hold up or if it will collapse again."*

I said, *"You cannot do this forever."* He replied, *"I agree, but I think we should continue for a while just to make sure."* That is when Karl stood up to him and said, *"I do not think so. Ever since the stroke, Patty nearly has panic attacks every time her bile duct needs to be cleaned. She always has a rough time. This is insane."*

I remember how Dr. Tzakis looked at Karl and said, *"Wait a minute! Who's the patient here?"* Karl responded with, *"We both are."* It was an excellent response, and Dr. Tzakis noddingly agreed.

He then said, *"To be honest with you, we do not know if it's the right thing to do, but let's stop it now."* So we stopped it, and my bile duct held up fine. I was excited about the fact that finally, everything was great. I was doing fine, but little did I know that another storm was on its way.

I really wished that the surgical fellow who caused the stroke, came and said, *"How are you? I'm sorry that this happened."* It's like it would not help a lot if he had taken responsibility. Instead, I felt like I was guilty of something because the hospital staff was treating me with kid gloves and showering love or avoiding me. It was clearly a medical error, and they did not want me to doubt that, but then no one could explain what had happened. I never thought I was going to see him again, but I did. It was many years later, and he looked at me and said, *"It is so good to see you look so healthy. That was the worst day of my life."* I felt like saying, *"Mine too,"* but I did not.

The Career Planning Event

Karl and I were at a planning event to celebrate transplantation. It was shortly after my stroke. A person from the hospital public relations was there as well, and Karl was still furious that they misplaced the central line. It extended my stay from one day to a month in the hospital, and we were getting huge bills for all the extra treatment. We just kept sending them back and said, *"We're not paying."*

Though the situation was not leading anywhere, we kept getting the bills again and again. We then talked to this PR person at the event and told her everything. However, instead of being sensitive to the fact that they almost killed me due to the misplacement that caused the stroke, this person actually told Karl: *"Oh Karl, you need to get better control of your emotions."* It was so incredibly insensitive of her.

In a situation like that where everybody was telling Karl that we needed to sue the hospital, it was more like fueling the conflict. I said, *"I'm not going to sue the transplant team." How can I sue people who keep me alive?* So, we went through that for a while, but I could not let them do that, it was ethically wrong.

People make mistakes, and that mistake does not make them the villain. We must remember when they were a hero.

Advocacy is Important

When I went to the hospital for my roto-rooter treatments, I had to go to the hospital's outpatient surgical area. It was the Jackson Memorial Hospital in Miami, in affiliation with the University of Miami. At that time, under the leadership of Dr. Andreas Tzakis, it was considered a leading transplant Center and perhaps the top for innovation. It was also the county hospital, which means everyone who did not have any insurance would also go to Jackson. I learned they would label our chart if we had private insurance. This suggested to me that if we had private insurance, we were supposed to be treated differently, which I thought was horrible. I really disagree with this practice. Everybody should be treated the same.

I did not know about all this until one time when I was waiting for my Roto-Rooter procedure. It was supposed to be at 8:20 in the morning. I arrived at the hospital in plenty of time, but it was of no use. The clock said, 9:30, 10:30, then 11:30, and my name was still not called out. About one time every hour, I would go up to the staff and ask the woman behind the desk, *"What was going on with the schedule down in the interventional radiology?"* Every time she said, *"They will call you when they're ready."* I said, *"Well, can you give me some idea of how long it will take, maybe I could go out for a walk or send an e-mail for a reschedule."*

She said, *"They will call you when they are ready, do not leave this area."* I was getting very impatient. That is when I called Debbie Weppler, who I must say is a wonderful person. Anybody going through a transplant or any other kind of major medical treatment, have repeated hospitalizations, and that is when they find angels in the system; Debbie was one of them. She was the transplant manager on the 15th floor. So, I called her and said, *"Listen, can you tell me what's going on. I was supposed to have my procedure at 8:30, and I am still waiting. Can you look at the schedule and tell me how backed up they are or whatever?"* She said, *"Well, I do know that we sent an emergency case down from transplant, which could be the hold-up. But they have several rooms. Let me find out."* She called, and she got me in, about fifteen minutes later.

The receptionist in the waiting room had seen me. She knew I was upset and she saw me on the phone. She called me back, and she said, *"I do not know what you did, but you can go back now."* So I went back to the registration area; they had their own registration area. I walked in and said, *"Why did it take so long, I was scheduled for early this AM."* She picked up my chart and said, *"This should not have happened because you're a VIP."* I said, *"What does that mean?"*

Then she told me about it, and I was really annoyed because nobody should have to sit there for three hours waiting for an appointment, regardless of what your insurance status is. I was really upset. Anyway, they registered me and got me set up with the IV. They took me down to interventional radiology then, and the doctor who was down there was one I knew very well because I was such a regular. He said, *"I hear you're causing trouble."* I said, *"Well, I guess so."* He said, *"No, I am sorry. You know, these things happen. But as an outpatient, you get put on the back of the list, and the inpatients are taken first."* I said to him, *"I got it. If somebody is acutely sick, they need to be attended first. I've probably caused many outpatients to be late because I have been sent down here many times. I understand it. But I think that hospital personnel could be more sensitive towards the patients waiting. Would it be too much trouble to let people know what is happening? Rather than just treating somebody like a name on a list and saying, go back there and sit, I will call you, they should inform each patient respectfully the number of cases before you, and so, you know that you will be seen later. Information is powerful; it provides us strength for the much-needed patience we need. I am not the only person who was annoyed and frustrated; no, there were a lot of them. I was just much more of an advocate for myself."* This is yet another lesson I learned through my continuous hospitalizations, advocacy is really important, but patience is also important.

I knew that I needed to respect the fact that people were doing the best job they could in the hospital, but at the same time. I wanted to be an advocate for myself because if I'm not, nobody else is going to be, and that's important to me. The transplant team in the hospital is really powerful. This was probably because in a public hospital like Jackson that has all these specialty units, they make their money off specialty unit patients. I get why they want the specialty unit patients to come back; that is because they want more private paying patients. Still, it does not give them the right to label people like that, and it was disconcerting to me.

You cannot always expect others to understand your situation

As I said at the beginning of this chapter, sometimes you have to listen to others and do what you are told without question. There are times this does not work out. One example: It is about time I had a procedure and threw up in the bed. I wanted to clean up immediately, but I was so helpless and had to rely on the staff.

I remember it was late at night when I returned to the floor from the procedure, after throwing up, I called the nurse and said, *"I just threw up."* She said, *"Okay, we will be with you shortly."* I was lying here in my own vomit for seemingly 15 minutes, helpless as the bed rails were up. I called her back up again. She said, *"This is in the middle of the night, Okay? We are trying to get a hold of the doctor. Would you be patient?"* I said, *"No, I have got vomit all over my pillow, and it's disgusting. How can I be patient?"* She said, *"We will be with you shortly."*

Believe me, I was annoyed to the core. At that point I could not get out of the bed because they had trapped me with the bed rails up. They were waiting to talk to the doctor just to see if he wanted to give me something for nausea.

That's why they did not come down. They did not want to make two trips down to see how I was doing.

Finally, a medical assistant came by. She said, *"Oh, why did not you call sooner?"* I had never felt so irritated in my life. I could have gotten up and just cleaned myself, or I could have walked up to the nurse's station and asked for another pillow, but I could not do any of this, and it just frustrated me. As I said earlier, when you are under critical care, you get locked in, you lose your autonomy, and you need to stand up for yourself when you need something!

The Beginning of Cancer

So here we go again! In December 2001. Karl and I were in Killington, Vermont, skiing with friends over the holidays. We were having a lot of fun, and in the middle of it all, I started to develop severe and unusual back pain. This was my first time skiing, and I was excited. Also, I was just starting to feel really healthy, so it was even better. I was on the slopes having a ball, performing miserably, but not caring when the pain became so intense that I could not tolerate it any longer. I hated to complain, hated to be the whiner, and hate to be the one always ruining all the fun, but I had to get back to the condo and lay down.

When I got back to Miami, I called my orthopedist. I told him something was wrong with my back. He examined me and took an x-ray. After checking up everything, he said, *"You need to get physical therapy."*

Soon, I went for physical therapy. The therapist said that he could not have me do the exercises since I was too fragile. He performed some cranial sacral therapy, and then he sent me back to my doctor, who then prescribed a strong anti-inflammatory to reduce inflammation. Just to be sure, he then said, *"Let's do an MRI."* Well, the MRI showed a mass with a 'likely malignant process' in my spine that had caused a fracture.

So, it turned out that I had a tumor growing in my spine that caused a spinal fracture. That's why I was in so much pain, and the last thing I should be doing was physical therapy. By March, I was fitted for a Thorasic-Lumbar-Spinal-Orthotic or TLSO, a brace that stabilized me from just below my armpits to the hips. It was designed to prevent my back from bending. The tumor in my spine was unstable, and any sudden movement could injure my spinal cord. I had to wear this contraption every day for the next eight months. It was so long as they could not figure out what kind of cancer I had. Therefore, they could not start the treatment.

Cancer is another one of those potential side effects of the anti-rejection medications. The most common is a non-Hodgkin's type called Burkett's lymphoma. The Epstein Barr virus causes it. The Epstein Barr Virus causes mononucleosis in non-immunosuppressed people, but it can cause cancer in immunosuppressed people. They gave me a medication called Rituxan, which is often effective and is not very toxic. They said, *"Okay, this worked for a lot of people. Let's try it!"*

From Sylvester Cancer Center to Mama Mia!

I was in the hospital for two days and a friend of mine, Lori Andersen called. She called on my cellphone, so she did not know that I was in the hospital. She said, *"I have two tickets to Mama Mia. You want to come?"* I said, *"Sure sounds good to me." "Can you pick me up from Sylvester Cancer Center?"* She was like, *"What?"* I said, *"I'm fine. I was just really wound up on prednisone."*

She came to pick me up, and I went to Mama Mia straight from the hospital. I was really energetic, and I had a great time there. On the other hand, the Retuxin did not work for the type of cancer I had.

Normalcy during cancer

I was presenting a paper in Stockholm, Sweden, at the World Federation of Operational Therapy that summer of 2002. I had to fly in my TLSO, and wow, was it uncomfortable. Many people thought I should not go; however, I had made a commitment, and I was really tired of waiting until the doctors figured out what to do with me. I really needed to get on with life! So Karl and I went to Sweden. The presentation went well, and the entire conference was something not to be missed, and I am glad I was there. I was in a lot of pain at that time. I was careful rationing my pain medication. I did not have enough.

Fortunately, arriving at the airport for our return trip, I guess they could tell that something with me was not right. They put us in business class, which was a lifesaver at that time. Sometimes really good things happen out of nowhere.

It was not the first time I got an upgrade because of things attached to my body, but it was a really fantastic opportunity.

As soon as I got home, I knew that I had to do something about it. I went to the doctor again. They did a CAT scan, guided MRI, and a biopsy. That's how we found out what kind of cancer it was, and then I had to go through the traditional chemotherapy and radiation. It was too much to take at the same time. It made me very weak and sick. There is only so much your body can handle.

Side Effects of Chemotherapy

Cancer had a massive impact on my life. When in the role of a patient, I learned that my biggest battle with myself was accepting when I had no control over myself and allowing others to take care of me. Yet, during cancer, I first experienced a time where I had to force myself into action when the time was right. During the time I was going through chemotherapies. Every day was like a challenge for me. It was getting more and more difficult as I was getting weaker with each passing day. For an independent person like me, it was murdering my self-worth. I remember I was lying on the couch at home one day, and I really did not feel well. My energy levels were at zero.

I talked to myself, *"Alright, Patty, you need to get off the couch, and you need to get things done."* Then I started talking to my husband, telling him that I have to get up today. We had an in-house pool. I said, *"I am going to go swimming."* He said, *"Are you sure you're ready to do that?"* I said, *"Yes, I am."* He said, *"Well, I'm not so sure."*

I was talking about wanting to do things, and Karl did not know what to do. He was sure worried, he said, *"I am going to call Lori and Carol."* Lori and Carol were friends, and they were both occupational therapists. *"Can you come over because Patty wants to do things that I do not think she's ready for."* They came over and tried to talk me out of it, but I was insistent that I had to go to the pool. Therefore, they had no choice but to help me get inside my bathing suit. We walked outside where the pool was, and they helped me to get inside. I am talking about the time when I was about 104 pounds and very sick. They kept trying to talk me out of it, but I was adamant that I was going to do this. It was only because I had to do something to satisfy my inner self, and yes, that helped.

I was tired of just lying down and doing nothing. When you turn from an active person who would never rest into a person who just could not move, you start to feel useless. It is the hardest thing to witness and most painful when you know you have so much to do in life. Anyway, I walked around the pool. I did not swim, but it was nice just to get out and walk, feel the warm water, feel the sunshine and the fresh air on my face. I was only out for about maybe three to four minutes when I started to feel tired. I went back inside and laid down on the couch again. I felt like I just laid there forever.

Unfortunately, it turned out that it was probably a bad idea because I became very sick, and later that night, Karl had to take me to the hospital again because I had a high-grade fever. I know it is frustrating, but you cannot let it get to you. I found I had to push through when people wanted me to be dependent. Then I got to a point where I felt like I was getting too dependent. It was easier to call Karl and ask him to get me this and that, but how long was that going to work? He noticed this as well that I was getting unnecessarily dependent. After a while, he said, *"Don't you think it would be a good idea to get up and get yourself that glass of cranberry juice* or whatever it is that you want*?"* He knew that I love cranberry juice. I started to think about it, too. Even though it was easy just to lay there and say, *'Honey, would you get me this?"* There was a time when I had to start getting up and doing things myself, yet, other times, it's okay to be dependent.

When I was in the cancer center, I had chemotherapy called CHOP. It was a very toxic therapy. I was very immune-suppressed because of the transplant medications. Every time I had CHOP, I ended up in the hospital. This was the second time I went to the hospital due to CHOP.

It was summertime in Florida, and despite the heat, I was so cold that Karl wrapped me up in a blanket and took me to the hospital. I could not stop shaking. They took me in a room and finally gave me something that calmed me down a little. A little while later, the nurse practitioner came in and gave me this long story about how chemotherapy affects my body. She said it was better if I knew what was going on with me and that I needed to accept these kinds of symptoms since they are common in immunosuppressed patients. I could see her, but I could not understand what she was saying. My brain refused to process any information. As a result, I did not remember anything she said, though I remembered who she was.

At some point that night, I do not remember when they took me out of that room and put me in isolation because my blood levels showed I could not fight infections. That is when the same nurse came in the next day. I recognized her immediately when she came into my room and said, "Good Morning." I said, *"I remember you from last night, and you told me everything about my situation. I do not remember any of it. Can you please tell me again?"* She started repeating everything from the night before. When she was done, I understood everything, she also said, *"You are in isolation. You need to wear a mask when you go out of the room, and it would be good for you to take a walk. Don't let your system get too weak."*

A little while later, I decided to take a walk down the hall. I saw that she was at the nurse's station with her back towards me, and she was talking to other nurses. When I got a bit closer, I overheard her talking about me and complaining about how I needed to listen to information, so she did not have to repeat herself. I was amazed that she was blaming me. Then she saw that I was there and I had heard all of this.

Later, I told her, "*Do you not realize that last night I was really sick, and there's no way I could have remembered what you said?*" She did not say anything to me; of course, there was nothing left to be said. My message – If healthcare providers really want us to learn, make sure we can take the information in writing with us.

Here is another lesson learned, you need to be sensitive towards people who are sick. You need to keep in mind, especially if you are a health professional, how that kind of sickness affects the ability to process information. I am sure I was not the first person who needed repetition. As patients, we need to be ready to ask questions and continue until we understand: to learn.

If you cannot remember things, write them down

At that point, I knew that I needed to stand up on my feet to find out things, and if I had trouble remembering them, I needed to write them down. It was also true that I had more medical knowledge than Karl did. Often, he did not know what was going on with me, especially with the cancer treatment and what kind of cancer I had. Still, we had faith in our Doctors and the hospital.

Because, over six months and three-needle biopsy's, there was still not enough tissue to determine the type of cancer, the doctors were arguing with each other over whether or not or to take me for an open spine biopsy. This procedure was not without risk and would require a substantial hospitalization and a long recovery. They kept giving us all of these options. We found it hard to process them. Every time we would leave the doctor's appointment, we would talk about all these discussions. Eventually, we mutually decided not to do the open biopsy, but it was so difficult to decide. I understand doctors need to let patients know these options, and I appreciate that, but it's tough to be in the middle of such a situation when all you experience is pain.

They had to take me off transplant anti-rejection medications because after the third chemotherapy, I was found to have no white blood cells. They were at zero. I was, therefore, kept in isolation in the transplant unit; they treated me there.

Dr. Harrington, who was my oncologist, came in, and he said, *"We have to stop your chemotherapy because you are not going to survive it."* *"Then what about my cancer?"* I replied. He said, *"Well, studies show that three doses of chemotherapy are very effective in treating this kind of cancer."* I said, *"Then why give me six?"* I was a little bit concerned because they only gave me three doses, and I knew I could not have anymore. They did a liver test, and it was a chronic rejection. They put me on anti-rejection drugs again. Dr. Tzakis, who is always there for me in good and bad, said, *"I guess you know that we have to change out your liver."* It made me think of taking my car for an oil change.

Angel in Disguise

You met some amazing people during your trips to the hospital, and my transplant surgeon in Miami was one of them. He was somebody who wanted to make sure that things were taken care of with his patients. He treated everyone as much more than just a patient; he treated them like humans. When my bile duct was closing up, I was unable to absorb any food or any nutrients from the food. I was not really interested in eating anything. The doctors were talking about maybe putting in a feeding tube called Percutaneous Endoscopic Gastronomy or PEG, where they feed you through your stomach using a tube because you are not eating. I was not interested.

Dr. Tzakis made arrangements for me to have a procedure done where they would do an external drain of bile duct so that it would be easier for me to digest food, and easier for my bile to get out of my system. He then said, *"Okay, that's done. But what can we do for you?"* He said that I needed to eat and get my strength up. It was so considerate of him because so many doctors will just take care of the procedures or write an order for catheter or medication or whatever the heck was needed. The doctors that actually spend the extra time, caring so much about the patient are gems. He was the type of doctor who was so sensitive to turn back and say, *"Alright, what are we going to do now to make you feel better?"* It shows that in that situation, I was more than just a liver. I was more than a broken bile duct, I was important. He was always looking out for his patients. He was great, but he could be very stern with the nurses if things were not taken care of.

When it came to me, Dr. Tzakis was always wonderful. At the time where they misplaced a central line and I had a stroke, he was out of town. He came back and immediately came to see me, *"I was out of town last week, and I'm really sorry."* He said, *"I should have been here for you."* I was like, *"Boy, you have to go out. You're an internationally recognized transplant surgeon, and I completely understand."* He said, *"Yes. But I hate that this happened to you, especially when I was not here."*

I remember another transplant fellow at the same time. His name is Jang Moon. He is now a transplant surgeon in New York. He was so kind and spent so much time with Karl and me, explaining what happened with misplacement of the central line, and helped to make sure that we were okay. He actually went over and above being helpful during that time. Dr. Moon was from South Korea and the Olympics were playing his country. So he told me about his homeland. When things like this happen you develop a relationship with these people, and all of a sudden, it becomes very difficult when you have another problem to deal with.

Who is really in charge?

When I was being diagnosed and treated for cancer, there were so many professionals involved that it made me dizzy. Everyone specialized in their trade, and so many doctors were treating me at a time that I felt as if nobody was really in charge. The transplant doctors assume the hematologist was in charge. He thought the orthopedic oncologist was in charge who thought the transplant team was running the show. This is another situation where you must advocate for yourself, you must.

I was going back and forth in treatments and dealing with doctors. At one point I became so frustrated that no one was taking care of my pain, I wrote an e-mail to all of my doctors saying, would you guys please decide who's in charge because so much is happening at once, and everybody, I think, assumes that somebody else is taking care of it

One of my doctors, Guy Neff, wrote back and said, *"I am so sorry. You are exactly right. Nobody is taking the lead with it. You come in tomorrow and see me."* He really helped facilitate the team doing what they did best to resolve that situation. He was another one of the really good guys, an angel in disguise I met in my journey. There are not a lot of real people who can visualize the whole process, so when you come across one, you just know it.

Getting discharged is yet another challenge

I also had to learn how to deal with people who always follow instructions precisely. These people have trouble using independent judgment. I remember getting discharged from the transplant unit after my first transplant. Being discharged is a nerve-wracking process because you're going home and losing all your support systems. At the same time, there is almost a chaos that you need to get through to be able to go home. They say that you will be sent home by 10:00 AM, then you are told that the resident has not written their notes, so maybe by 12:00 PM, you will be released. After that you need to be cleared by the education nurse who arrives at 2:00 PM. So by the time you finally get discharged, you're just really frustrated and annoyed. All you want to do is go home.

I still had another hurdle to deal with. The nurse educator came in and said, *"I have to go through all your prescriptions, and make sure that you know your medication and know-how to give yourself insulin."* I said, "I'm not diabetic. I do not take insulin," and she said, *"Well, I have to make sure that you can independently give yourself a shot before you leave. It's on the protocol."* I said, *"No, I am not going to give myself a shot. I do not take insulin, and it's not necessary. So let's just skip that one."* She was still insistent, *"No, it's not going to happen,"* I said.

That is when Debbie Weppler came in, and she said, *"She does not take insulin. She does not have diabetes. Can we just get rid of that education point?"*

She was like, *"Oh, yes, of course, we can."* The important thing to remember here is that things should not be this difficult for a patient, especially during the frustration of the discharge procedure. It was hard.

Summing it all...

I had no guidance in learning how to be a patient in a hospital and I do not think most other people do either. As an occupational therapist, it was both an eye-opening experience and reinforced a need for learning. I was a therapist for about 20 years before I became a patient. During the 20 years, as an occupational therapist, I have always thought of myself as client-centered. I hope I always consider their viewpoint and values.

I realized that sometimes we need to be paternalistic towards what a person wishes to do or get done. It's all about how you communicate with them and find out what they need or want. What is it that would make them less stressed out? Being at the hospital is very depressing and very stressful. I do not think health care providers always remember that.

I had a primary care physician. As I got sicker and was nearing transplant, I had a lot of questions. She said, *"I cannot deal with you as a patient."*

I asked why, to which she said, "You ask too many questions. I do not have enough time to answer your questions." I said, *"Well, can you book me for a double appointment?"* She said, *"No, I'm too busy, and I cannot deal with all of your questions. There are too many things that you want to know that you are not my specialty."* She never said, *'I do not know the answers.'* She just put it all on me.

The next thing she did was get a piece of paper on which she wrote names and cell phone numbers of three other doctors for me to contact because they were taking patients. It was hard to go to another doctor and explain your entire history starting from zero. It is terrible.

That was when I realized that I needed to make a timeline. Hence, I made one that explained all about myself and what was happening with my body. The doctors really appreciated that and still do, especially in times when I just have a sinus, headache, or something minor similar to that, and they want to know my history. It can be really confusing for you to explain all over again, so that timeline helped a lot.

I learned through my experience that the doctor would come by a couple of times a day when you're in the hospital. I would think about things that I wanted to ask him. At first, I got confused when the doctors came in because I had forgotten by then what I needed to ask. Therefore, I started writing down everything. I would literally hold my list, and ask the doctor one by one. They appreciated my organization.

Many people may think it is crazy, but my experiences have made me a better person. It really has enriched my life because it not only helped me personally but professionally as well. The lessons helped me be a better therapist and a better educator. They also helped me to be more responsible for myself and take care of things as soon as they show up and not wait for somebody else to be there or get them done. You need to keep in mind that the medical system in our country is fragmented to the core, and it is so because there are so many different aspects to it; it is vast. Many doctors are doing so many things and dealing with countless people regularly, so I always remind myself that the only person who keeps up with everything about me is me. I learned this the hard way, but pretty quickly. You need to put yourself first, not waiting for what everyone else has to think, say, or do.

Chapter 10
Transplant # 2

When the doctors informed us I needed another transplant, Karl and I were in shock. This was the last thing that we expected. I was still recovering from the first transplant, a stroke, and chemotherapy, and here I was, being told that it was not over yet. I had to be strong, and I had goals, things I wanted to achieve. I was not ready to allow my life to wither away. Moreover, there were so many people who cared about me; my family, my friends, colleagues, my students and Karl. He deserved to get past of this and finally live his life; our lives. Hence, I knew that I needed to get it together and do it again. Little did I know what was ahead.

Taking life in stride

Before I found out that I had liver disease, my life was quite in order. Things were very predictable; they could be called routine. Soon I had sensed that something was just not right, but I strongly believed that my health was under my control. I told myself that if I ate right, regularly exercised, and took care of myself, I would stay healthy when in truth, I would not.

I struggled with actually believing that I was sick. Therefore, I continued to think I was healthy, look forward, and act positively rather than being caught up in all the worry and doomsday predictions of what could happen to me. Call it denial; I did not want to focus on it because I just did not want that to be my life, and I did not want to succumb to being a 'Patient' to accept the role of being sick.

When I look back today and think about it, much of my belief that illness is sometimes perceived as weakness, and as a young female professional, I had to be strong, I believed that if you focus on being sick and weak, then you lose credibility. I did not want any of that to happen to me, so I chose not to focus on my illness and not to complain.

Nevertheless, I soon found out that staying positive and pushing my illnesses to the back of my mind, was not going to make them go away. This was to be my life. I learned that I needed a second transplant in January of 2003. It had been five years since I was hospitalized for HE during my father's funeral. During that time, I had a transplant, three years of regular rotor rooter treatments, a medically induced stroke, and spinal cancer, which took ten months to be diagnosed and treated. Karl and I lived our lives driving back and forth to the hospital. It seemed like nothing was helping – not enough.

I am the type of person who believes that you should ask for help if you need help. Although, in my case, there was nothing that anyone else could do. I had convinced myself that whatever was happening in my body, if I just tried hard enough, I could control it. I found out that it was not going to happen.

Thinking back, in the early 1990s, I attended a lecture that I could completely relate to. It was at the American Occupational Therapy Association, and the lecture was from Susan Fine, the Eleanor Clarke Slagle Lecturer. Her topic was resilience[5] or one's ability to mentally or emotionally cope with a crisis and return to pre-crisis status quickly. She discussed how some people are resilient, but many others are not. Many references involved people who survived the Holocaust and rejoined life, as opposed to people who did not. She talked about the people who lived their lives

---

[5] Fine, S. B. (1991). Resilience and human adaptability: Who rises above adversity?. *American Journal of Occupational Therapy, 45*(6), 493-503.

afterward. She said that they either allowed themselves to lament their misfortunes perpetually or they accepted unpleasant experiences and moved on with their lives. The idea of moving past difficulties towards one's goals resonated with me. Some people went after life, while others lamented their past and waited for life to come after them. In my experience, if you wait for life, it never arrives. This is just how this world works. You must work hard for what you want, and for me, I always went after life.

First VS Second Transplant

Let's step back and get a bird's eye view of both my transplants. With my first transplant, I waited six weeks for the transplant, and with my second, I waited for six months. During the first transplant, I was quite strong and had been working and running right up to my transplant. Heading into the second transplant, I was wasting away; down to 104 pounds. Each time, my body reacted very differently.

At the time of the second transplant, I had a whole bunch of different problems going on. I had just finished cancer treatment, and that was really hard on me. That was the reason I lost a tremendous amount of weight.

During the nine months of waiting for the second transplant, I was getting sicker and sicker. Dr. Tzakis called and asked Karl and me to see him. He wanted to discuss the possibility of accepting a liver with an "O" blood type, instead of the "B" I needed. By that time, I had done a great deal of research about transplant compatibility and incompatibility. Karl and I went to meet with him, and I admit I was hesitant. Hence, I declined the offer because I understood if I accepted it, there was a risk of rejection and incompatibility involved. Even though it was not a huge risk, I knew that with my second transplant, I had to be very careful to get a strong liver, for my body was already going through a lot.

The Pilot Program & Second Transplant

In August of 2003, Karl and I received a call from the transplant unit. It was Debbie Weppler. She asked if we would be willing to be on a pilot television show being shot for the A&E network about transplants. She said they were looking for four different people who were likely to be transplanted in the next several weeks to be on this show. Karl and I did not even have to think, we immediately said yes, because we were interested in promoting transplantation and telling the world what it was all about. After that, she asked if we could come down to the hospital so that the producers and the TV crew could interview us to see if they were interested in our story.

We went down to Jackson Memorial right away. My first question was, *"Debbie, does that mean that I am going to get a liver in the next two weeks?"* She laughed, *"Well, we hope so, but there's no guarantee."* Anyway, we went down, and the television crew interviewed us, and they were just amazed by our story. They said they would get back with us, so we went back home.

The phone rang shortly after we got home. I picked up, and it was the TV crew again. They said, *"We would like to come up to your home and do the interview this afternoon. As a matter of fact, we are on our way now. The studio in Chicago is interested in starting soon."* Karl and I rolled our eyes at each other. I was ready to go to bed for a nap, and he was getting ready to go to work. We had to cancel everything because this was important to us.

They came over soon after and started the interview. In the middle of the interview, my phone rang yet again. I picked up, and it was from the hospital. They had an organ for me. I can never describe my exact feelings in words after hearing this news. My feelings of happiness being able to get another transplant were mixed with fear of another transplant. They told me afterward that they knew there was a potential organ available, and that's why they had to come over right away and match the interview with the time I got the call. This way, they captured an intensely emotional scene with us getting the call and getting ready to go down to the hospital again.

The crew followed us down to the hospital. As we went through the admitting process, we had this camera crew behind us recording everything. I was already being paid a bunch of attention, but they knew we were coming before we got there. The camera crew filmed every single thing. I went into surgery, and that's the last thing I remember for about the next seven days. I completely blanked out.

My surgery was quite difficult, and I learned much more about it than I ever wanted to know while watching the TV show afterward. It was traumatizing to watch. I heard and saw things that I should not have, like Dr. Tzakis saying that he knew to go in there would be a 50-50 chance for me to survive this surgery. I do not know if I wanted to know that. Of course, he did not tell me that before the surgery, because what's the point? A doctor never wants his patient to be scared, but even more, I would not live much longer without the surgery. As I mentioned earlier, death was not an option for me. Watching the television program, for me, was an emotional experience. I still get tears in my eyes if I watch that show today. Karl will not watch it. It brings back too many memories. I believe that they ended the documentary well with an encouraging message for all the transplant patients out there, urging them never to lose hope. It was 24 hours of film, and they took the most intensive and emotion-laden 15 minutes for each of the four transplant recipients. I must say they did a commendable job.

Post Second Transplant

What came after my second transplant was certainly not something I had expected. Afterward, in intensive care, I became so sick that they kept me mostly sedated for four days, probably because I was in and out of surgery. I had a lot of things going on inside me at once, and those things needed to be repaired. Though, I have no memory of any of that time. Karl was always with me, and mostly by himself. That was until my sister came. In ICU, I apparently tried to fix her up with Dr. Tzakis. I said, *"You two should go for a date while you're here. You would get along."* She said, *"Well, what about my husband?"* I said, *"He could go too. You three would really like each other."* When I made sense, I would crack silly jokes to lighten up the mood because I started to feel that everyone around me was seriously concerned about my health. I honestly do not remember any of my time in the ICU.

You all must be well aware by now that I am not the kind of person who can stay in one place for a long time. I cannot. Apparently, I asked Karl to get me out of the hospital and just take me to lunch in South Beach so I could get a break. Also, I wanted to eat some sushi. I assured him that we could get me back in the hospital in time; no one will even know that I had left. Of course, lunch did not happen, but many such things happened during that time that I had no memory of. Afterward, when I found out about those things, I realized that I was rather entertaining and a challenging patient in the ICU.

Because of people like Doctor Tzakis and his right-hand nurse Debbie Weppler, Karl, and I were well aware of our situation and knew exactly how to proceed further. As much as it helped me, it also helped Karl to make sure I received the best possible care.

Many others helped in innumerable ways. I was incredibly fortunate that Kathy Sweeney Whisler, my best friend in Jr. High and High School, lived close to me. She was a dedicated friend and companion. Michele Adams Michaels, a great friend, and former housemate who was also a nurse was very involved. Michelle told me later when they brought me out of surgery, she rolled me over and felt for any surgical tools that may have been underneath me.

These are type of good friends to have. Michelle and Kathy helped in so many ways. It was the same time my mother needed to be in a memory care unit. It was 2003, and her Alzheimer's had progressed to the point where she was no longer safe at home. While I was in surgery, my sister Joanne was in Hingham, looking for a solution. She accessed all the senior care resources, trying to find live-in-help. She was unable to ascertain that she would be taken care of and there were just no family who were close, so they took the next best step.

After my father died and my mother was still healthy, I asked her what her wishes were, and if she had to leave her home. She was adamant, *"Patricia, I do not want to leave my home."* So we discussed it as a hypothetical potentiality. She finally said she wanted to be in Hilton Head with Michelle and her grandchildren. So, my brother John flew down with her to Hilton Head. I was so frustrated I could not help, and my siblings had to deal with this alone.

While we had to deal with my illness, I was only confronting my ailments while my husband not only battled with my health but also with my doctors and me. He met a lot of different doctors with considerably different demeanors. There was a doctor during my stroke who told him to prepare for the worst. Karl describes that doctor as a totally heartless being with no human compassion. Then there was a self-absorbed professor we met at the radiation center where we sometimes had to wait for five to seven hours. If we complained, he would coldly respond, saying, *"It takes time."*

When my student became my therapist

Days were passing by, and I was still living in my head. My body was weak. I did not want to get out of bed. An occupational therapist came up to my room, and it was a former student of mine. I said, *"Hi, how are you doing?"* She said, *"Fine,"* and we talked for a little bit. She then said, *"I am here to get you out of bed."* I told her that, *"I am sorry, I am too sick. I am not getting out of bed, come back in a week or so."*

I was going against my own teachings, but my brain was not working at that time. In school, we had taught our students how sometimes patients would be very resistant to getting out of bed and doing certain things. We taught them techniques to use to get people up because research has shown that early mobilization is healthy for people in the hospital. She, however, just turned on her heels and walked out the door. She did not try to talk me into anything. It is important to note that she did come back.

I did not want to get out of bed. As a patient with such grave problems, you likely never want to get out of bed. You feel miserable because everything you do hurts. Every movement hurts, and the idea of getting up and walking around is simply the worst even though I knew intellectually, that's what I should be doing. Therefore, I gradually started to get myself up, and I was taking short walks. I was doing everything that I was supposed to be doing, but boy! It was not easy.

One special quality of Karl

I think this chapter is becoming too serious, so let's take a moment to appreciate Karl's special quality. I was in ICU for about seven days, and I was then on the floor for another 30 days. That's just too long, too long for anyone to be in a hospital bed. You just feel so weak, and as much as you walk around the hall, you start to feel even weak. Karl stood by me during that time and was always there to take care of me.

Once they removed the nasogastric tube and I returned to a regular diet, Karl brought me a home-made lunch and dinner every day. In case you don't know, Nasogastric tube is a tube which is passed through the nose and down through the nasopharynx and esophagus into the stomach. It is a flexible tube made of rubber or plastic. Usually it is placed after a surgery. It can suction fluids put of the stomach or put substances into the stomach, such as nutrients when a person cannot take food or drink by mouth.

Even at the beginning, when I had little to no appetite, he still brought me food. He understood when I could not eat it. When I was able, he would serve me meals in the lounge area, which meant we sat at a table. While our home was only about 20 minutes away from the hospital at the time of my first transplant, this was not the case during the second one. We had moved in the meantime, and now we were 45 minutes to an hour from the hospital. None of it mattered to Karl, though.

At that point, the transplant staff knew us very well, and it was funny how they were always so curious about my lunch and dinner. Karl had come to be known for bringing food into the unit. He was often asked, *"Karl, what do you have for Patty today?"* Truth be told, everyone loved whatever he brought for me, so this became a reason why everyone was always asking him what's for lunch and what's for dinner. Karl was so generous that he would even bring in treats for the nurses. It surely was a very special quality of Karl, his ability to cook. He knew how to win hearts, and this is how he was able to bring me food, even when I told him he did not need to.

Being a Patient

As I said earlier, being a patient was never on my to-do-list. No one ever expects to be a patient, but when it hits you, things get hard. During a time when there was great emphasis on providing evidence to support actions, procedures, and treating treatments, my illness occurred. Naturally, I was always curious to know everything about my disease, and why I took a certain medicine or went through a certain procedure.

Because I was a health professional, I was given a lot of choices, a lot of information which I wanted. However, being a researcher, I could not necessarily process all of that information without looking things up and asking lots of questions. I think that most of the doctors, nurses, and other professionals really appreciated that. Although sometimes they used to get annoyed by my continuous series of questions, they said, *"Patty, would you be quiet and just do what you need to do?"* (in a kind way) I never took any of that personally as I knew that I could be demanding and had no control over my curious soul.

This is what happens when your life takes a turn, and everything all of a sudden is upside down. One serious illness, followed by a prolonged recovery, can rob a lot of things in your life. You end up losing things you thought you never would. You witness many major changes in yourself and around you, and those changes are not always pleasant.

People start to treat you differently; they show sympathy when they have no idea what you are going through. Everybody has a bit of advice about what you should be doing or what you should not be doing. Basically, you need to reassert yourself in the life that was yours before the transplant. Of course, you now have a list of things to include as there are things that you do differently now, like have transplant labs done once a month and watch what out what you put in your stomach, take your medications every 12 hours without variance as prescribed. You must watch and make choices about what you are going to do. Your life revolves around intentional living and being specific. You have to take charge of yourself. I always found that I was able to pick up the pieces of me.

People do not really know what an impact they can have on your life while you are at your weakest. They often highlighted changes that I had not considered. For instance, I would see people, and they would say, *'Wow, you look great,'* then the next time, *'Wow, you look so much better.'* I understand people want to be supportive. However, through their comments, I started realizing how awful I must have really looked at the beginning. And, truthfully, in the beginning, I most likely did look awful. I was gaunt, pale, all skin and bones, and it showed on my face how much effort it took to do the smallest task. I was back at work as soon as possible after every episode. My work was important, and my students were my responsibility. The point was— however I looked, it was always me in there!

Going Bald

The changes my body was going through were sometimes really difficult for me to handle. Going bald was one of them. I went through three episodes of losing my hair, and believe me, losing your hair is an unpleasant experience. I always reminded myself that it's just hair; it will grow. I never wore a wig. I would sometimes wear a hat, especially going outside in the Florida sun. Other than that, I did not really try to cover up my bald head.

I went *completely* bald only once with chemotherapy; the other two times, it was just major hair loss. After my first transplant, I lost a lot of hair around the temple a well as the hairline upfront; it kind of looked really scraggly and unhealthy. My hair was falling out because I had been sick for a very long time, and my body was weak.

To start with, I had a lot of thick, curly hair. With chemotherapy, when my hair all started to come out, I was about 70% bald when I went to my hairdresser and had it buzzed. It was salt and pepper as I had been coloring it. It didn't bother me as much as it bothered so many other people. My brother Fred wanted me to wear a wig because "*I did not look like me.*," it bothered him. I was surprised how many people reassured me it would grow back. I actually liked it. I wore it very short and grey for ten years. Then I decided to let it grow out. It got to a point where I either needed to color it or cut it short again, and I colored it and again and let it grow long. Then after my bout with autoimmune pneumonia, it was falling out, so I cut it short but still colored it. On my website[6] there are many pictures of me with different haircuts and colors- that is me! Most recently, with the COVID situation, I could not get it colored for three months, so when I could finally see my hairdresser, Carley, she just cut it real short, and now I am grey, nearly white! I like it! The only thing that concerned me was, *why does it have to be my head where it's so physically obvious?*

The scars were under my clothing because they were on my belly and legs. They are not visible most of the time. My hair loss was something that got attention. I was not as uncomfortable as other people. I just had to figure out how to deal with this so that people would not focus on my head.

Forgive my digression – back to the story, this time, it was very difficult for Karl as he was stuck with a whole set of new roles. He was responsible for taking care of me. He made sure that I had everything I needed. And at the same time, I was not doing well with mine. I put work as a priority. I would go to work, and I would come home with no energy left for anything else. I used to get so tired that I would go to

---

[6]patriciajscott.com

bed early. I had no productive energy to contribute to any of the house chores.

The thing is – I had fewer roles to play at that time, the most important one was that of a patient. Karl had multiple roles to play; he played the role of a husband, the role of a caretaker, the role of a doctor, and he was the home maintainer and the role of a caregiver. I used to get stubborn; sometimes, he would talk me out of things that probably were not good for my health. Karl was stuck with me in that situation, but he never complained, not even once. He changed his life, and he did everything in his life according to the perspective of how it would affect my life. I really hated the fact that I was consuming his energy and time. However, he had moments where he had to force himself to get through the day during many difficult and frightening times. However, he stood firm and was always kind and persistent in his actions.

In one way or the other, I was influencing his identity. He was unable to surge forward and take control of his future for a long time because I was so dependent on him. I cannot even imagine being the caregiver of someone going through such a serious illness. On the other hand, I have tremendous respect for people who do not have supportive family, friends, partners, or spouses. Although I have not experienced this myself, I have met many transplant recipients for whom an estranged sibling, an old friend, or even a support group have become their solution. Supports come from amazing places when we are open to them.

The important thing is that you have to want to get better. It's so important to have the will. I had the will to live and just get over the phases where all I did was lay on the bed all day. I will always be thankful to the people who stayed kind to me during that time. Being a patient was not easy, but it sure taught me the value of life and that of people.

The Recovery

The second transplant was way more complicated than we had anticipated. Cancer treatment was testing me at every step, and during our sessions at the cancer support group, I would often hear Karl saying that he would much rather have another transplant than go through the cancer treatment again. Today, we feel very differently. After the second transplant, I was in the hospital for five weeks due to complications. Despite the long hospitalization, difficult surgeries and even longer recovery, has worked out well. My reflections on this are that despite the difficulties we endured.

During the first transplant, I had problems afterward, but after the second one, very few. Although the recovery took a long time, it did pay off. The number of hospitalizations after my second transplant has been minimal. Though the second transplant had lots of risks, it paid off very well in the long run.

After my second transplant, I was hyper-vigilant about any potential problem, and I was hyper-responsive as well. Because of that, I feel that my recovery was more thorough and smoother. As I was physically getting better, I struggled with my confidence. I had to keep encouraging myself that everything would turn out right because, at that point, I did not know when the next shoe would drop. It would not be wrong to say that the emotional recovery took longer than my physical recovery.

The lesson I learned is it's important never to give up, no matter how difficult the situation is or how much you feel that things are never going to be the same again. No matter how confusing things may be, just know that everything will fall in place. Life constantly resets. Things tend to have a way of working out; we just must persist. I knew I had no control over my disease processes, all I could do was keep on moving towards a desired future, and what I wanted to accomplish, so I did. I never had the sense that I was done, and this was it for me. I wanted to move forward and discover what was going to happen next in my life. I was looking forward to the day I was finally free. I was tired of being sick, and I desperately wanted to be healthy again. I did not want any more of that, and the hope of good days kept me going and helped me recover.

I will close this Chapter with another poem my brother wrote for me during this time.

Blessedly for you

I want you to know
As I pray every night
I ask God to bless you
And keep you from fright

I ask God to bless you
And keep you up strong

RESILIENCE

Shower down blessings
All the day long

The angels are with you
Wherever you go
God's infinite love
If you are high or low

God bless you and keep you
From losing your way
Building up confidence
As you work and play

God bless you and keep you
From negative thinking
Look up to the heavens
God's eye will be winking

God bless you and keep you
Inspire your mind
To grow to your fullest
Be gentle and kind

-John Charles Scott Jr.

Chapter 11
The Chaos in the Mind

I was in a cage. It was a cage made of four walls, and it was not the only one. There were other cages with animals in them all around me. The animals were taken out of their cages and into a room at the end of the hall. I tried to call out to people around me, but no sound came out of my mouth. I was sure they had forgotten about me. I sensed I was invisible to them. I was there, but nobody could see me, hear me, or feel my pain. I was in line, waiting for a liver transplant; they simply could not ignore me. However, I was sure they had forgotten me. This was not the hard part.

Periodically the walls of the cage would start to close. The cage would tighten around me and continued to close it until it crushed me. I tried to scream to get the people's attention all around me, but no sounds would come out of my mouth. It was as if somebody either set me on mute or the people around me were deaf. The pain was excruciating, and it was constant. Then when I was sure I could handle it no longer, the walls of the cage would release, and the pain was gone. The moment the pain let up, I had a huge sense of relief. I was still trapped, but at least I was okay. Suddenly the walls of the cage started to close in on me one more time, and that continued until I was crushed again

How many times did this cycle repeat itself? I have no idea. All I can remember is that at the time, it seemed endless. How long did it last? I have no clue. Maybe a minute, maybe seconds, maybe fractions of seconds. I have no idea. In my recollection, it was hours. It is when I was in Surgical Intensive Care for a week after my second transplant. My theory as to why these hallucinations happened after my second transplant was the length of time I was on morphine. I have had morphine before but never for this long. It was the fifth time in as many years that I was in ICU.

Chaos is a state of extreme confusion and disorder, and these are the exact words that describe my condition when I was in ICU. It was tough. My experience was different every time, every day, and every moment because my levels of awareness and levels of pain during specific times were different.

The Hallucinations

The first of the hallucinations, where I am in a cage, was the first hallucination I had during the time I was in the Intensive Care Unit. It was a difficult, horrible, and painful period. I no longer knew what was real and what was just in my head. The hallucinations were one of the side effects of the morphine. The very first real memory I have after my second transplant is going back up to the 15th floor; the transplant floor. I remember looking around and thinking, *"Oh, since the last time I've been here, everything has changed. They have now decorated the room in this shabby chic."*

One of the things to remember here is that I had been there many times before, and I wondered why they put in new flowered curtains with valances. I wondered why they put a dresser and creative rehabbed furniture. I was not sure why there was a group of gypsies in my room. The woman in the bed had a transplant, and her whole family and their entire clan were camped out next to me. I could not figure out what was going on. I do not know how long I had been wondering. At some point, Dr. Tzakis came in and said, *"Okay, Patty, what's going on?"* He said, *"This is the first time I have had a husband of a patient call me and say, 'I think my wife is overmedicated. She's not answering the phone. She's not making any sense. I do not know what's going on with her.'"* That's when I found out that it was all in my head, and apparently, I was hallucinating.

After that, they moved me to a private room where there would be fewer distractions so I could work on myself. I am not really sure if this was a solution to protect the other patients or me. They said I was too sick. Certainly, I was sicker than they realized I was. At Jackson Memorial Hospital, they had a hall with double rooms on one side and single rooms. We did not usually get sent to a single room unless we had a real strong infection or if our immune system was really weak, and we were very sick. That's when we would go to the other side of the hall. I had been on the single side of the hall before. I was there for the rest of my stay.

It was quite a confusing time. Later, the doctors found out that I had full-blown Morphine psychosis. I had other kinds of hallucinations as well. I remember being in a hallway, and there were several other people, and we were all liver transplant recipients, lying on stretchers. We were all waiting to go out to this large gathering of people who were celebrating transplantation. We could hear all the speeches, but they never could find us to bring us out, and none of us knew why we were there. I remember waiting in that hallway for hours and hours during that celebration. We never got there, and it was so frustrating as it went on and on in my head. I found it horrifying and confusing at the time. Now I realize it was a toxic effect of morphine.

Hurricanes and residual cognitive events

When I was out of the hospital, after my second transplant, I could feel there was a lot of stuff still going on. Also, it was hurricane season in the outside world.

There was a period I was going back and forth in terms of my health. I was still cognitively messed up, but I was doing okay. I was taking notes during one hurricane where we lost power. I was writing down everything I witnessed or felt. The storm hit Hollywood very badly. It was bad enough to keep us without power in a major metropolitan area for about a week, but it could not be compared to Hurricane Andrew's devastation, for example, in 1992.

During the hurricane, I have this notation of how I was looking out the window. We had hurricane shutters, and just one was made of plexiglass so we could see out from our kitchen window. The rest blocked all views from the outside. I was watching the roof tiles on my neighbor Rommey's roof, as they were just peeling off in the hurricane-force winds. I thought, *"Wow, that's really interesting."* I did not know that this could happen and felt bad for Rommey and his roof. Karl came up to me and said, *"Do you know Patty that if that's happening to Rommey's roof, it's probably also happening to ours."* I said, *"Yeah, good point."* It was not too much longer before we heard a big thud, and the whole house shook. There was a tree on our roof.

If you have never gone through a Category 1-5 hurricane, the problem is there is a long lead time coming up to it where you wait to see if you are in the cone or not. Then if it looks like you are in the cone, you batten down all the hatches. The last thing you do is close the hurricane shutters. Typically, once you do, there is no sightline to outside. Then if the power goes out, which is really a question of when, not if, you find yourself in a dark space surrounded by winds, howling, and things being blown around, including trees and shutters and anything else not nailed down.

We did not go out at that point because the hurricane was still moving through. When everything settled down, Karl went out. After a while, I could hear him up on the roof. I could hear him, and at the same time, there was a conversation going on inside my head. A voice inside me said, *"Oh, Karl's on the roof. That sounds so fun. Why do not you go up and join him?"* On the other side of my head, Kevin said, *"No, that's probably not a good idea. Why do not you just stay where you are, while Karl checks out the roof,"* and then I again found the first voice overruling the latter, *"Oh come on. Go up on the roof that would be fun."* It was like two guys, say, Jim and Kevin, *debating in my head. "Karl will be really upset with you if you go up on the roof right now,"* Kevin said again. I literally named the two voiced Jim and Kevin. I did not remember that until I came across the notes that I had written during the hurricane.

Thoughts about drug-induced psychosis

In surgery, and afterward, for pain, many drugs may cause toxicity in the brain, which manifests itself in a delirium state. In this state, patients may experience an altered consciousness and even hallucinations, illusions, and or delusions. This altered state is transient, meaning the person may go in and out, and it is not permanent. There is an important difference between hallucinations, illusions, and delusions.

My experience in the cage, where I could see the sides coming in to crush me, and I recall the pain, is a hallucination. It was sensory. I could see the sides come in; I could feel the pain. A hallucination is a sensory experience not based in fact. The most common type of hallucination is auditory. With visual and other sensory types, there is usually a toxic cause.

A delusion is an irrational belief. It is fixed and not based on reality. An example could be a belief that every time blood was taken for a test, that much blood was lost and would not be replenished. This belief cannot be changed through information or knowledge. With a delusion, the belief is persistent against logic.

An illusion is a miss-interpretation of real external stimuli. The person sees something that is real and misinterprets it. Perhaps they are semi-asleep, and the wind is blowing the trees outside their room. The shadows may appear as though someone is moving back and forth outside. Any of these phenomena can occur with altered states, and I have experienced them all.

"The only true wisdom is in knowing you know nothing."

-Socrates

Part III
Moving Forward (mostly)
2005-2020

Chapter 12
Recovery and setbacks

We have all heard that things get worse before they get better. I did not understand this statement before I got sick. Now I do. When I got sick, I thought that this is it; I will handle it, and my health problems will be over. Then I realized things would never be the same again. There were times when I thought I will not be the same Patty ever again. That was not entirely true. If not the same, I got a lot better as an occupational therapist and even better as a human.

Life has a funny, harsh way of teaching you things, but when you realize it, you feel much more aware of the world around you. I never imagined that I could learn so much from my disease. My experiences have taught me a lot of things, and I am more patient, accepting, and tolerant today because of all I have been through. I will always be grateful and proud of who I am today. I am glad that I did not let my disease become my identity, and I am proud that I finished my Ph.D. and continued my work as an educator despite being sick.

I have experienced many physical and emotional changes throughout my journey. I have tried to put them out in this book for readers to benefit from my experiences. After I recovered from the disease, I decided that I would ease others' suffering by making the information available for them. Let us first look at the changes I observed in myself:

I have become more empathetic

I remember once when I was in my 20's; I was co-treating in a pre-discharge group with a colleague, a psychologist, with patients on the psychiatric unit. After every group session, my co-therapist would always say to me, *"Patty, a little empathy would be good."* She tried to explain to me that when someone says they have to go home, they do not know what they're going to do with their life after all this is over and that they do not know what's going to happen to them, you do not have to jump in and say, *"Well, what are you going to do about it? What are your plans?"* She asked me to think about, at minimum, starting with, *"Well, that must be difficult..."* and then *"what are you going to do about it."* I used to tell her, *"Okay, I'll try."*

Despite all of this, I always found myself caught up in, *what are you going to do about it? What am I going to do? What is the plan? How is a certain thing going to be taken care of?* That is when I realized that I was more rational than emotional. I am always interested in the solution more than acknowledging the impact of the problem itself.

Although this did not work in some situations, it did help in others. At that point in my life, I was the occupational therapist in the psychiatric unit and the cardiac care unit. In the cardiac care unit, patients either had to change their lives, or they were going to die. This left a room for being honest, and you could be direct with them without beating around the bush. This was always easier for me because I am very direct and straightforward. This was the scientist in me. I could quickly tell them that you should do this, you must find a solution to resolve this or else you are not going to survive.

Return of Health Does Not Mean Return of Life

Early on, one thing that stuck with me was the stress of being a patient on top of doing the important things in life. Not that maintaining health is not important – it is of utmost importance. Without our health, physical as well as the mental aspects, feeling, and thinking, we are not ourselves. I became concerned about how others who, without any medical background, try to cope. I was concerned about the problems they faced and the ways they were suffering and how little they understood it – and what they could do about it.

For example, there was a time when my bilirubin was high, 11.8 mg/dL, to be exact. One of the transplant surgeons, Tamaoki Kato, saw me walking in the hall and guessed it to be at 11. Normal is 0.0 mg/dL – 1.0 mg/dL. The ducts in my transplanted liver were blocked, and the bile was entering my bloodstream. I needed a new liver. This is when the transplant surgeons and interventional radiologists got together and presented me with an option to keep the current liver, a desirable outcome since there were no other livers available.

This option required several surgeries and led to the repeated rotor rooter treatments, the ones I had to endure every month for 3 years. It was a difficult decision yet my trust in my surgeons enabled me to agree to the procedure. I understood there were no guarantees.

That is when I started writing a paper 'life as an N of one.' As a patient, I learned one important lesson: it is important to be well aware of your own situation to be an advocate for yourself. You must know about all the procedures, medications, and survival information that is communicated to you and always question if you do not understand something.

Doctors would come to me and say, "We just wanted you to know that 42% of people do better with this medication. Do you want to try it? Or you need to know that 80% of people do just fine with this procedure, and 23% of patients survived the disease." I would always turn back to them and say, *"I do not care about the percentage; right now, I care about what will happen with me?"* – Selfish? Yes. Helpful? Not really.

I possessed much information and held the conviction my life was going to be okay. I needed more control over evidence-based information to understand the impact and/or consequences of an action. I wanted to be able to grasp the impact of what would happen in my life and my situation. I needed to feel better about myself. I wanted to be aware of all the possibilities. That is when I got into doing a lot of research into what happens after liver transplant and the personal factors that influence recovery.

There is a caveat in my argument. It is important to recognize the predisposing reasons for transplantation, and the residual problems may very well present major impediments to independent living. I will argue here that that one should never exclude the opportunity of living life to the fullest. Very often, individuals who struggle overcoming challenges need the services of an occupational therapist, a clinical social worker, or a psychologist.

How My Research Began

I have always been inquisitive, and I always liked to have insights into everything that goes on around me. I never liked wasting time; I always need something to do. Therefore, when I used to be awake at night due to the disease, I would get online and try to discover autoimmune hepatitis and HE. Remember, I am talking about the time from 1996 to 1997, the World-Wide Web was not what it is today. There was little information available online, and it was not much of a help for my understanding.

Back in 1998, I found that there was not much literature about transplant recovery on the internet, and in published research, there was no literature on what people could do to change their situation. There was an international study that 39% of people would go back to work and live their normal lives. I was like, okay, what about the other 61%? What happened to them? I was always curious.

I wanted to find out whether this 61% of people: 1) decided not to return to work; 2) were too sick to go back to work; 3) were retired; 4) had some other primary role such as home maintainer, or caregiver, or 5) would like to work but faced other barriers. This led to a lot of the studies I did with my students and colleagues over the past 20 years about recovery and survival. We were able to identify some of the factors that make the difference in a person's recovery journey.

One thing that became obvious in the review literature was that people who decided to retire early lived with poorer quality of life than the people who went back to work and enjoyed retirement at the expected time. Some studies show people never recover from their helplessness from being a patient, which, in my opinion, is not just right. Everyone should be able to live their lives to the fullest. The people who were able to return to work and perform other primary roles, such as being a home maintainer or worker or volunteer, showed a better quality of life, as compared to those who retired earlier than planned. My opinion is that this can be compared to waiting for the train to come and hit you, or not. Come on! Anyone who has had a lifesaving transplant or any lifesaving procedure has been given second, third, or in my case, a fourth and fifth chance. In my opinion – this is another chance at life! Not just survival!

I would go on what was called "bulletin boards" precursors to websites and Facebook. Yahoo mostly hosted them. Yahoo had many topic-specific discussion bulletin boards, and I was on them for a long time until I found other sources to connect with people and collect information. One thing that was evident from my personal research was that nobody knew a lot about these topics. Because I found little to nothing, I vowed to devote myself to researching post-transplant recovery so that others would not have the same problem. This is how my transplant-related research career began.

I was able to get access to evidence-based clinical studies because of my academic position. Back in those days, you had to find a journal related to the subject you are researching about. Yes, you had the choice to search online to find the article, but then you had to go and physically get a copy of it. I had access to university and medical libraries, which helped me a lot, and so it was not a problem for me to gain access to journals.

I remember attending a lecture by a man named Dr. Charles Christiansen. He was president of the Occupational Therapy Foundation and a scholar in occupational therapy. He talked about how some people languish, and others surge forward after suffering from an unfortunate challenge and very little in the middle.

This led me onto a path in my research to answer the question; what is the difference between somebody who would do that and somebody who would not? I wanted to get first-hand information, so I decided not to ask the patients when I had the opportunity. During my research, I have met hundreds of transplant recipients. I remember talking to a kidney transplant recipient one time about what he was doing after the transplant. He said, *"Oh, I'm resting my kidney. My daughter donated her kidney to me, so I am not going to do anything to risk losing it."*

Serendipitously, his daughter was one of my students in the occupational therapy program at Florida International University in Miami, Florida. I knew her, and she was certainly not the kind of person who would want her father to sit at home for the rest of his life. So, I said to him, *"Do you think that she would really want you to do that?"* He said, *"No, she does not. But she does not also realize what it would be if I lost it. So I really have to take care of it and cherish it."* I understood his rationale, but his decision to become a couch potato and gain weight is not the right way to take care of your kidney.

Therefore, with his permission, I talked to his daughter, and the two of us were able to talk with him. He made a couple of changes in his lifestyle, but he really did not make significant changes.

Again, this experience helped me focus on the problem that is successfully treating the medical problem, meaning you return to your health, but it does not necessarily mean that you return to life.

In 2016, I was awarded the Bantz-Petronio Translational Faculty Research award at Indiana University at IUPUI for my research in helping transplant recipients return to a productive life. As a condition of the award, I had to give a lecture, and the title of it was *'Return of Health does not mean Return of Life.'* The whole idea is that the intersection between being healthy and living a productive life is a better and more desirable outcome than simply survival.

Years ago, the benchmark of success in transplantation was the survival of the patient's transplanted organ and the patient. It is way past that because most people who undergo transplantation live afterward, it is just a question of how long, and increase of the quality of life saved. This is a positive development as nobody knows how long they're going to live. However, each individual needs to make the most of the time they are given on this planet.

My goal was patient empowerment to support a positive identity. Obviously, immediately after transplant surgery, when you are healing and getting healthier to focus all your attention on the role of a transplant patient. You need to do exactly what the transplant team tells you to do. You must follow all the instructions and take care of yourself. But do not lose your true self in the process. As soon as it is comfortable, you need to take responsibility for yourself and not be the transplant patient, but be the person 1) you were before the transplant happened; or 2) the person you desire to be now, for now, you have a second chance at life. Start to move back into a new normal. This normal will incorporate the routines and habits you now have to maintain the health of your organ, and your job, your social and family life and the other valued roles you have. Do not let the patient role overwhelm you and limit your life. This limitation is similar to sitting in a cage for the rest of your life. It takes courage to escape that cage, but once you do, life will be so much better, and you may uncover new ways of living. Ways of living you only dreamed about.

Life after Transplant #2

After the second transplant, everything at the hospital was so difficult that Karl and I came home with the jitters wondering what would happen next. It had been about six years since we got married, and two months later, we entered into the first transplant, and we were just unsure of what was going to happen next. For the entire span of our then 6-year marriage, he had been my caregiver. During that time, I cared very little to participate in household and day-to-day decisions. I recall one day he said to me, *"You need a new car. It is time."* I said, *"Okay,"* he then asked me, *"What type of car would you like?"* *"I do not care."* was my response. A few days later, he asked me if I had thought about it. *"No, I do not really care. Will you pick it out?"* This time Karl was exacerbated, *"Okay, I will look around."* He did, I approved, and the first time I drove, I ran a red light and had a very large dent. But that's another story.

After the second transplant, things went very well, which was the opposite of what we expected. This was this first time in years that we started to settle into a reasonably normal relationship and were happy about it.

Later that year, I had a large incisional hernia, which needed to be repaired. It was my last surgery in the year 2004. I was thinking in my head that this was just the start of another series of hospitalizations in the upcoming years. Fortunately, I was wrong.

At the start of this book, I discussed 'advice.' Immediately after a transplant, or in the recovery of any serious medical condition, you will receive advice from people. Consider, evaluate, revise, and accept or reject. Make it your decision.

The Messy Research

I remember there was a time when patients were making decisions about their health without knowing the consequences. In 2009, President Obama gave a speech at the American Medical Association. He spoke of how patients are making decisions without the benefit of information. He said it was the responsibility of health providers to explain and the evidence to support that information.

I was also teaching Evidence-Based Practice at that time, so that was influential in my way of thinking. The essence of my research was resilience, which gives one person the ability to overcome the challenges of returning to full participation in life... and another who does not. In the research field, it's sometimes referred to as messy research. It's not straightforward, and there are so many factors which in humans are hard to isolate and measure. For instance, a clean question is: how many cases of flu will this vaccine prevent? The outcome is measures by viral load. The kind of questions I was looking at were much more complex: How many people will go back to work after transplant? The answer is more complex, did they work before transplant? Is work only paid employment? What about caregiving and parenting? So many human behavior factors and the environment impact the basic outcome variable.

From Miami to Indianapolis

After a few years of no more incidents, we realized that we were safe to leave our medical caregivers in Miami. We had developed such a strong sense of confidence in the doctors and nurses that we trusted very much; we knew we could call on or rely on them no matter what happened. They knew my medical history, so I did not have to start from scratch in case of any kind of emergency. We wanted to leave Miami, but we would lose this whole network of the medical support team that we had developed. It was a big decision.

In 2007, we decided that we were finally ready to leave Miami. We wanted to move to an area of the country which had four seasons. We both grew up with four seasons, and that's how we wanted to spend the rest of our lives. Miami is beautiful for sure, but we had to move on. The next question was that if not Miami, then where? To be able to decide where we were going to move, I started looking for another university position. I was in a tougher position to relocate than Karl, and Karl was wonderfully willing for me to direct the move location. The two of us would make the final decision, but I took the initiative.

If I talked about my desires, I was looking for a university with a strong departmental leader committed to the program as I did not want to be the chair of the department anymore. I wanted to be able to teach and productively do my research.

Karl and I looked at a couple of places together, and we short-listed three places. Occupational Therapy Academics are a small professional field, and I knew a few people in each of the short-listed programs. The location that we selected was Indianapolis. I was unsure. Growing up and living mostly by the ocean, I never really thought I would want to live in the middle of the country. Although I lived in Oklahoma for ten years, I preferred living in coastal areas. I just really like being surrounded by the ocean. We looked into the three options, Karl and I both traveled to a beautiful Northwest coastal region which we loved, an eastern mid-Atlantic area near the coast, and then to Indianapolis. We realized that everything about the position in Indianapolis was just perfect. It met all of my criteria, so we knew which option we were going to choose.

Anyway, there was nothing that could stop me at that time. I chose Indiana University due to the proximity to Indiana University Hospital, where they had one of the largest, by volume, liver transplant units in the country. A lot of my research was done through research mentoring of students. I was successful in obtaining internal university funding and had a good deal of internal support. Since I taught research and supervised students in research, we always had some really interesting projects going on.

I started recovery studies in Florida. It was complicated to transition from being in the role of a patient, especially one who was in the hospital so often to the role of a researcher. I personally felt the difference, and I am sure the staff at the hospital felt the difference too. I could never really separate the two.

This was one of the biggest reasons I wanted to move somewhere else to make a fresh start and be able to separate the two roles. At the same time, it was very difficult to gain access to researching a transplant unit. The transplant team is very protective of their patients. They impose lots of restrictions because patients are typically very sick and highly immunosuppressed. Unless you are authorized, outsiders have no access to the transplant unit. The staff does not want their patients to be exposed to any emotional and physical stress because they are already going through a lot.

The biggest advantage of the Indiana program was that the head of the Indiana program was Joe Tector, Ph.D., MD. He was one of the transplant fellows when I was a patient at the University of Miami, Jackson Memorial Hospital. Dr. Tector knew me well, so I had a good chance of gaining access to research. Moreover, Dr. Tzakis wrote a powerful letter to him in support of my ability to do research. Hence, I was able to get access to the transplant unit, which was huge. Research in this field was something I was very passionate about, and everyone could feel the energy I was putting out in this cause. The doors kept opening for me, and I could not be more grateful.

Interestingly, for me, this was another clash of roles. As then an Associate Professor of Occupational Therapy and an Adjunct Associate Professor of Surgery, my credibility was established with health professionals and researchers. Some of these same health professionals and researchers, when they learn about my role as a transplant recipient, would question my credibility. However, when I would introduce myself to a potential research subject as a former recipient of not one but two livers, my credibility has heightened.

I could literally walk into a room with my white lab coat on. I looked like any of the other doctors or other health professionals. I have my badge on. I would introduce myself and say, *"I would like to talk to you about a research study on recovery."* The patients would kind of roll their eyes on me and avoid the conversation saying they were not feeling so good.

Then I would say, *"I understand how you are probably feeling right now, but the reason why I am interested is that I have had two liver transplants, and I want to help people going through this,"* and that's when I would get all the attention I needed. The patients would open their eyes, look at me with curiosity, and boom! I have all their attention.

This is so because I was credible to them. I have been in their shoes. I was not just another person conducting research. I have gone through the pain and the uncertainty they are suffering. Therefore, they would participate in the conversation enthusiastically, and that is how being a transplant patient myself helped me on my way to conducting research.

I faced many barriers to getting funding for my research. In academia, you must bring in the money to support your research. The university holds you accountable for the way you spend your time. I wrote multiple federal grants and found the priorities included increasing the number of people who donate organs and medical treatments to prevent organ rejection once transplanted. Survival, and quality of life is not the kind of research that was fundable at that time. It is typical of our societal focus on medicine and not on health. I think this is changing, and issues of people living healthier lives are getting more attention through the PCORI initiatives. PCORI stands for The Patient-Centered Outcomes Research Institute, which is an independent, non-profit research organization created to help patients, and those who care for them make better informed health decisions.

This time I had to start on my own without any support. I moved to Indianapolis in August of 2007, because I needed to start teaching fall 2007. Karl stayed in Miami because 2007-2008 was when it seemed like every other house in Miami was for sale, so it took us a whole year to sell the house. Also, we did not want our house just to be another vacant for sale house. So, he stayed back until it got sold, but we did not realize it would be eight months until Karl got to Indianapolis.

He was finally able to join me in April of 2008, and during that time, I stayed in a month to month furnished apartment. It's not that we stayed apart for the whole time. Every two weeks, he would come up, or I would go down to Miami for a long weekend. We would visit each other regularly but did not get enough time to spend together.

An unexpected turn

It is about the time when Karl and I were looking forward to spending a solid two weeks together. It had been a long time since we had. I had time due to Christmas break, and I flew to Miami. Unfortunately, the day I got to Miami and was ready to settle was when my mother took a turn for the worse. She was on Martha's Vineyard, and her condition was critical.

Fortunately, I had spent a week at Thanksgiving with her, so I felt good I had that time with her. It burned in my mind that my incredibly wonderful mother struggled with so many losses; Alzheimer's and Parkinson's disease together. I did not feel the need to rush out. I knew my mother was dying, and she did pass away the day after Christmas. It was fast and at Christmas. It was heart-wrenching for me to see my mother struggle, but even more heartbreaking to find out that she was no longer around. I flew up right away to help my sisters and brothers make the arrangements for her funeral. Karl joined me after a few days, and I said good-bye to the most beautiful person in my life. I still often think of her, particularly when I see a beautiful sunset, a beach, an exquisite flower, or just in everyday moments. I miss her. She died too young.

Karl sold the house, and we brought up the rest of our belongings and two cats to Indianapolis in March 2008. It was interesting that we closed on a home on April 1, 2008, in Indianapolis. Our closing of the home in Hollywood, Florida, was April 1, 2000. We also met on April 1, 1991. There has always been something about April Fool's Day and successful events for Karl and me.

A litany of problematic side effects

Anyway, we settled in, and everything was going well. I tend to forget that people do not know that I had two liver transplants, survived cancer, and had a stroke and other medical issues. I did appreciate that I had left all of those back in Miami. However, I needed to construct a new medical team up here. I started with a primary care physician.

I still remember my first appointment with the primary care physician. We were talking and going through my medical history. Hearing all of the things he looked at me and said, *"Why are you still working? Do not you think after everything you have gone through, you need a break?"* I looked at him and said, *"No. I essentially missed six years of my professional career, and right now, I am looking forward to having the opportunity to make it up, because there's a lot of things that I want to achieve."*

Hearing all of this, all he said was, *"You're amazing. You do not need to do that."* I said, *"Of course I need to do that. This is what's important to me."* So, we continued with the discussion of my health, but this first meeting was surely not so pleasant for me. He shortly after left to take a position in another facility, so I never really got to spend too much time with him. I then switched to a different primary care physician. However, I always remember his reaction after hearing my medical history. As a physician, he would be encouraged that medical science has done so many positive things, but instead, his reaction was disappointing.

Anyway, this did not take much of my attention because I had a lot of other things to do. I had to set up a new hepatologist, a new neurologist, and a new hematology oncology physician because of cancer follow-up. I had lots of people on the list that I needed to put in the sight because I left Florida with a functioning liver, but I had lots of scars and very real medical needs.

I should clarify that the neuropathy results from the distal nerves dying from chemotherapy. These aftereffects cause lots of problems with your feet, primarily coldness and pins, and needles. I also had terrible balance problems after the stroke, including a sway while standing to lose my footing and stumble. It looked like I was drunk! I still suffer from this problem. Another problem was terrible handwriting. My handwriting was poor, to begin with, and the stroke made it almost illegible. My students would come up to me, *"Dr. Scott, what does this say? I cannot read this word."* Even I sometimes could not read it.

Nevertheless, I had a clear head and a great outlook for the future. I really was excited to be in Indianapolis, continuing with my teaching and research. I was grateful for the opportunity I was given, and things were looking very positive.

Though I had minor things here and there, the most important was monitoring my transplanted liver. My foremost physician was my transplant hepatologist, who followed my medications and my labs and would communicate with my transplant physician in Miami. My progress was good. I was happy. I was getting physically stronger, swimming regularly, and working out in the gym. I was also doing well at work, and my research at the transplant unit was taking off.

Research on Recovery and Return of Health

I began by making contact with pre- and post-transplant people and looking at the experiences they had in the process of waiting and/or recovery. I would start by asking questions and using two assessments[7] to explore areas such as how long it would take before they could start to live independently and feel comfortable with it, cook a meal, or feel comfortable climbing stairs and getting dressed. Having been a patient, and I know from experience that resuming these activities takes a while and for me, at least, fatigue was a big issue. This is how I started my transplant research, and this research was very fulfilling as I collaborated with the physicians, the transplant staff, and, most importantly, the occupational therapist. Emily Winslow Sanders was one of my graduate students who completed her research on the transplant unit and then became an employee at the hospital. Emily was an invaluable colleague. I learned to understand the constraints of integrating this work on life issues while meeting the traditional role expectations of the occupational therapist on the team. Let me explain.

---

[7] The Role Checklist Version 3 (RCv3) and the Occupational Self Assessment (OSA) and – OSA Daily Living Skills Scales. Both available from the MOHO Clearinghouse.

My perspective is that the occupational therapist on the inpatient unit FIRST needed to focus on helping patients understand how to cope with basic daily living activities. They would need to help patients plan for life when discharged from the hospital to their own home so that they could get in and out of their own bed, on and off their toilet, and in and out of their shower. When you have a huge painful incision in your belly, something as simple as getting in and out of a chair becomes difficult.

The program enhancements we developed came from the needs assessment from interviewing many patients and recipients. This was a 4 Phase program. Phase 1 was initial data gathering, Phase 2 was data collection about recovery patterns challenges and successes, Phase 3 was program development and testing, and Phase 4 is next. Phase 4 is the translation of the revised program modules into a manual which will be available to other transplant centers and for individuals. My writing of the transplant recovery manual is in line directly after this book is completed.

The content of the programs falls into areas of rebuilding routines. Eating and making healthy choices, at the same time returning to responsibilities, work and other productive activities. Resuming social and recreational activities, emotions and stress, and so on.

Patients and their families were very interested in this work. So much attention is paid to the waiting period and surviving the surgery, that people often forget about the difficult and prolonged period of recovery. The ability to perform Activities of Daily Living is an essential precursor to returning to role participation. For example, you cannot go to church or lunch with friends if you cannot shower, dress, and get in and out of a car.

One person in particular that I got involved with is a transplant psychologist. Her name is Dr. Audrey Krause. Interestingly I met her at a neighborhood get-together. Lisa, who was hosting the party, is a mutual friend. She said, "*Oh, you two probably know each other; you both work together.*" Dr. Audrey and I looked at each other and did not recognize each other at all. Then she said, *"You both work in the field of transplant."*

This was the beginning of a long and deep conversation about transplants. After about an hour, my husband came up, and I introduced him to Audrey. He said, "*Did you tell her about yourself?*" I said, *"No, not yet."* She looked at me strangely and said, *"What have you not told me about yourself?"* I said, *"Well, I was getting around to this. I also had two liver transplants."* She looked at me again and said, *"No, you're kidding."* I said, *"No, I'm not kidding,"* and the conversation continued for another couple of hours. What we did not realize was this was the beginning of a very strong friendship. I now count her as one of my best friends. We have talked endlessly not only about transplants but about life and about other things. She has been a huge support for both Karl and me.

The undissolved stitch

No matter how much you try to move on, your past follows you everywhere. After the repeated problems I had dealt with, it was obvious that things would never be the same again. It kept showing up at different points in life, and never in my control. By this time, I was pretty much known on the transplant unit as somebody who was doing research.

One day, I was in the outpatient clinic doing research consents with patients and ran into my hepatologist, Dr. Paul Kwo. I told him about this bump coming out of one of my transplant scars. It was very sore and was beginning to bleed

PATRICIA J. SCOTT

a little bit from time to time. He said, *"I think you know what that is, it's an internal stitch that was supposed to have dissolved, and it has started to make it through the surface."*

That is when I discovered that the stitch, placed ten years earlier, had not dissolved. He said, "Let's see if we can get this out." He told me to go upstairs to the transplant unit, and that he was going to call Tony Davey, a nurse practitioner on the transplant floor. Dr. Kwo wanted to see if Tony could take care of this or if he needed to have one of the residents pull that stitch out.

As I was told, I went up the transplant floor and found Tony Davey. At first, he was like, *"What? You're a transplant recipient?"* Tony knew me as a researcher. I just assumed everyone knew about my past, but I was learning this was not true. I was finding more and more people did not know, so I was not surprised by his reaction. At that time, my concern was the undissolved stitch. I immediately replied, *"Yes,"* and one of the residents came in.

He tried to pull it out, but well, it was impossible. We ended up having to schedule a surgery to take that stitch out. It had been in there for over ten years now. After the number of surgeries I had dealt with, this was nothing big; a few hours. I was done with the surgery, and after a day or so, I went back to work and just went on with my life. This is what I meant when I said I always had a few minor things going on here and there, other than that I was doing well.

A trip resulting in autoimmune pneumonia

In the year 2017, I had a huge step backward. In November of 2016, I had taken ten of my graduate occupational therapy students on a service-learning trip to Belize. The trip was well-organized, and everything went extremely well. It was a wonderful learning experience, and we had a successful trip.

The trip was organized in such a way that there were two days of decompressing and just relaxing on one of the islands off the coast of Belize, which was exciting for the students. They got a chance to unwind and enjoy being relaxed because they had been working hard.

One day we went snorkeling on a barrier reef. I am an excellent swimmer, and I have a lot of experience in snorkeling, so I had no concerns. At one point, I dove down, came up, and cleared my snorkel. At least I believed I did. I took a deep breath and ended up inhaling a bunch of water.

After that, I started hacking but did not think anything about it.

I went back to Indianapolis, and it was about two weeks later that my health started to worsen. I developed a cough so severe that I went to the faculty staff clinic to get myself checked. After checking everything, they told me that I was fine. So, I went back home, and about two weeks later, I was in the hospital with pneumonia. They ran all kinds of tests, but they could not figure out what was wrong with me. They sent me home on a dose pack of steroids and antibiotics.

Christmas or Christ-Miss

Two weeks later, it was Christmas, and my family was coming to our house to celebrate that year. My brother John had arrived first. He arrived with a horrible cold, so much that he went to an urgent care clinic, where he got the care he needed. I was not doing very well either, so Christmas was more like a Christ-miss. I have not mentioned my brother John very much. He is the silent partner in the family. John played a significant role in my recovery, not by being around, but by being available. As I mentioned before, we would spend hours talking on the phone. John writes excellent poetry, and he wrote of my situation. He also is a fabulous storyteller with a great sense of humor. I love nothing more than someone who laughs out loud while they recount an excellent story.

Most of the family were there, but the joy was missing. Hospital appointments replaced the celebrations. There was one event I insisted on following through – a Christmas Eve afternoon party. My sister Michelle strongly urged me to cancel it. She assured me my friends would understand, and she was right; they would have. However, in the usual form, I insisted we went on with it. It was a bad idea. Although it was a lovely party, the stress I placed on my family to get through it was unnecessary. We were surely missing out on one of the best festivities of the year, but that was not the concern. No one was even thinking about it.

I had had trouble breathing ever since I came back from the trip. I went to see my primary care physician get to the root of the problem, and he said, *"You are not breathing well. I will have you go down in the emergency room and get the pulmonary tests and x-rays done, so we have a clear picture in front of us."* Tada! I ended up getting admitted again, the last thing I wanted at that time. I was admitted for a while, for they could not figure out what's wrong with me. As a result, I was sent back home again about a week later. The whole week of Christmas, I was severely sick, but with my family there, we somehow managed to have a good time.

Another turn for the worse...

In the first week of January, I had another appointment this time with Dr. Lacerda, my hepatologist, at the transplant division. I barely made it to his office, which was in a clinic at the hospital. I did not realize my condition was so obvious until I walked up to the desk, and the nurse said to me, *"Are you having trouble breathing?"* I could not utter words at that time, so I just nodded in a yes. She called somebody right away.

They took me into a treatment room and checked my oxygen, which was at an alarming rate of 80%. Dr. Lacerda came in to see me right away. Now, he is one of the kindest, most caring physicians I have ever met. He is also incredibly smart and intuitive. He looked at me and said, *"With an O_2 level of 80%, and by just looking at you, I need to admit you right away."* They got me into a hospital bed, checked my lungs, ran their tests, and after a bronchoscopy, the doctors came back and said, *"Your lungs look like cottage cheese, they are full of gunk."* The news did not surprise me because, by that time, I was having trouble breathing even with oxygen; it had to be something. They then moved me to what they call a step-down unit, which is a level below the ICU where they put people who are critically ill, needing things like pressurized oxygen, and close supervision. They ran all types of tests for bacteria, viruses, and fungi, trying to figure out what was wrong with me. It was a terrible time, and I just kept getting sicker and sicker day by day.

I felt so helpless, I did not know what to do, and the doctors were perplexed. Every day I was visited by three different teams: The Pulmonary team, Infectious Disease team, and the Transplant team. The Hospitalists who admitted me were there too. The nurses were terrific. It's one of those units where you have a nurse and an aide assigned to two rooms, so they constantly check on me and make sure that everything was fine and that I was getting enough oxygen.

Cryptogenic Organizing Pneumonia

After staying in the hospital in that condition for a couple of weeks, it got to a point where I started to think that I was not going to survive. One night when Karl was leaving I said to him, *"I do not know if I'm going to be alive tomorrow morning when you come back."*. We said heartfelt and tearful good-byes. Shortly thereafter, Dr. Audrey Krause, whom I mentioned earlier, came in. Being a psychologist, and my friend, she knew at that point all she could do was just listen and let me talk. I talked as much as I could. I let out everything I felt was happening, and she was a great support. She was a support for Karl as well. They were friends, and it was beneficial because, again, Karl went home unsure of what was going to happen next, whether I would be there when he comes in the morning or not. Moments like these are very depressing, and for a spouse, it could not get any worse.

Fortunately, later that night, one of the pulmonologists came in and we started conversing. He said, *"We have tried everything till now; the only thing left is prednisone."* He then said, *"I am putting it off because if it's viral or bacterial, prednisone is just going to make it explode."* When I asked him what exactly I am suffering from, he said, *"Well, it looks like you might have something called cryptogenic organizing pneumonia, which is a rare autoimmune syndrome, an inhalation pneumonia."* It turned out that was it; this was what had been causing me so much pain and suffering. I knew it happened because I had inhaled the water. I recall when hacking cough began. Although there was nothing wrong with the water, it was saltwater off the coast of Belize; it was the fact that a foreign substance was inhaled, and that triggered autoimmune pneumonia. I was put on a high dose of steroids.

Recovery

By the next morning, I was about 20% better, and by the following afternoon, I had made about 50% recovery. My pulmonologist came in and said, *"You look wonderful."* I said, *"I know. Can I go for a walk?"* He said, *"Yes! That's fantastic. I'm going to call one of the physical therapists, and they'll take you out for a walk."* I said, *"I'm going to be out of here by Friday."* It was a Wednesday. He said, *"I do not think so."* I said, *"Yep, I'll be out of here by Friday. I know how fast prednisone can work for me,"* and it did turn out that I was right. I was able to go home and continue the process of recovery. I recall it was the day of Donald Trump's inauguration as our 45th president. Waiting for discharge, I watched the whole thing on TV.

Earlier that morning, they did a test on me to see if I had to be sent home on oxygen, and fortunately, no, I was free. I was free to go home without any chains. It was 2017, 20 years since this ordeal had started. 2017 was a long year for me. I remember when I came back home in late January, I used to sit in a chair in the living room. I would spend most of my time in that chair. Even getting up from that chair was not easy for me. I could not get my breath. Even to be able to go to the bathroom, which was not too far away from the chair in the living room, I had two extra chairs placed on the way to get there.

If I did not have enough breath to make it through to the bathroom, I would sit down and restore myself. This is only one way in which my occupational therapy background helped me. This is how I was recovering and surviving. My students would come and visit me because I would help them along with their research while sitting in my chair. Amy Bercovitz, my research assistant, my right hand while I was in the office, came by regularly. I felt good whenever they came in; at least I was productive somehow.

The longest course of prednisone

In Chapter 3, I talked about prednisone. Treating the Cryptogenic Organizing Pneumonia, Prednisone again saved my life. However, it was not going to be a short-term solution. I was told I would need to take a high dose, long-term steroids. I started on 60 mg/daily for six weeks, 40 for six weeks, 30 for six weeks, 20 for six weeks, and so on until I was finally off the 2nd week in September. This time I had every possible side effect of this medicine. A photograph from the graduation party with the students that went to Belize shows how blown up my face was. It shocked me when I saw it as I never thought of myself being that altered, I was getting better, and from the inside, I was the same. My body was just getting used to breathing when I was surprised by the news of spiking blood sugar. It was 500 at a regular blood draw on February 2, 2017, for transplant labs, believe me, this was totally unexpected and quite a shock!

During the next couple of days, I went from never being concerned about my blood sugar levels to testing it every day when I woke up, before every meal, and before bed. My blood sugar levels would determine how much insulin I would take using a Humalog Kwik pen, short-acting insulin during the day, and Lantus, long term-acting insulin at night. Only once did I confuse the two and took way too much of the Lantus. I immediately realized my mistake and looked up the impact on my computer while trying to get in touch with the nurse on call. By the time she got back to me, I had eaten a bowl of ice cream and half a box of Girl Scout cookies. I had to stay up for 4 hours and check the blood sugar every 20 minutes to make sure it did not get too low. She laughed and said, *"You will be okay, but fruit would have accomplished the same thing."* This is not a mistake to make.

I did not return to work until April. In the beginning, I started coming back part-time, and then I realized I was facing a problem. Since I was still not healthy, I would need a 20 minutes nap right in the middle of the day. I thought of going back home, but at that time, it hit me that I needed to be asleep, not driving home because once I had a nap, I could come back to work and could concentrate. So, what I did, was instead of going home, I brought one of those inflatable mattresses to work. It was propped up behind my door.

Whenever I felt like my batteries were getting low, I was able to take my naps and charge myself in my office. I would set my alarm, close the door, and shut off the lights. Then I would nap for twenty minutes, and it worked like magic, I would wake up feeling a lot better.

Probably about a week later, after coming back to work, my boss and the chair of the department told me that he was going to accept the position as a dean at another university and asked me if I could take over in running the department. Now, I was still sick, and I knew that it was a bad idea, but I also knew I was the only one in the department qualified to do it. If I did not do it, an alternate from outside the department would fill in until the position could be refilled. And, that was a risk. If I did not do it, then the department would be at the risk of losing accreditation while not having a qualified chair. Therefore, for the sake of my department, I said, *"Yes, I would."*

As I had expected, it turned out to be the wrong decision. I still had a lot of time before being fully recovered, and the position of chair of the department is very demanding. So, that was not a good decision for me, nor was it good for the department. The faculty was expecting me to perform at the level of the prior Department Chair. Under general circumstances, I could, but in my compromised state, I just could not. I was forcing myself through each day because I was committed to doing it, I signed up for it, and I could not just back out until they had another option. The wait was long; the faculty was frustrated with me. However, it was worth it because, a year later, we hired an excellent chair, and she's now doing amazing things while I am happily retired. Hiring her was a great decision for the department as well as for me. A bonus for me was that she was a student of mine at Florida International University 20 years before.

Up to that point, I still felt like I had not gotten enough rest and did not give myself enough time to recover. That last episode of pneumonia really made it clear to me that I had over 20 years now since I was brought back to life because my first transplant took place in 1998, and if I had not been transplanted, I would not be here. I believed in myself and never gave up. I was an active and firm believer that I was going to be healthy again. It took a lot of strong will and physical efforts to believe that, but it paid off for me to allow me to be strong and live a good life.

This long term course of prednisone hastened the deterioration of my bone density. I had been diagnosed with osteopenia when I was back in Miami, and during the ten years in Indianapolis, I had a bone density study every two years, and I was holding on my own. Well, this stopped after the last course of prednisone. Despite my yearly infusions of Reclast to strengthen my bones, my last bone density study moved me into the category of osteoporosis.

This impact of the prednisone on my musculoskeletal system appears not to be limited to my bones. In 2018, I was evaluated for a bicep tear and had to have 3 MRI's from three different MD's before anyone decided to make the diagnosis. You see, 65-year-old women rarely tear the bicep tendon. That privilege is assigned to male weight lifters. So, after many missed diagnoses (the story of my life), I was scheduled for Bicep Re-attachment surgery.

The surgery went without a hitch. Amazingly, my rehabilitation, which was scheduled at Indiana Hand and Shoulder Center, was to be done by several of my prior students. My primary therapist was Deana Bodkin. Deana was my research assistant in 2014. She was instrumental in the 4th International Institute's success for the Model of

Human Occupation, an International Occupational Therapy Conference I hosted at Indiana University at IUPUI. She was also a co-author of a research publication. So, Deana was an important person to me, and to put my rehab in her hands was fantastic.

There were several other former students there also including Jessie Salley. While Jessie was a student, her graduation research involved implementing, testing, and revising and revising my recovery program for post-transplant recipients. I spoke of this already. Publishing this work is my next challenge.

Post-discharge, all transplant patients need to visit the hospital once or twice a week to check their medical progress. This program is designed to assist in the transition home, and the readiness to return to productive living. Jessie was incredible for this project as she is creative, enthusiastic, and pays attention to detail. Most of all, she is a people-person with an ever-present smile. So, while my rehab team was great, my recovery was not. I developed heterotopic ossification, which is excessive bone growth at the site of the biceps reattachment. The heterotopic ossification's impact was that it interfered with supination, the ability to turn my palm upward.

So, the saga continued. This was just another example of a potential adverse side effect of the surgery, which less than 5% of people get. That would be me.

Karl's Career and Indianapolis

Before we moved to Indianapolis, Karl was successful in the wine distribution business. Although we were both ready for a move, the decision to go where I could find a position to further my career again meant he had to compromise his career for me. Wine distribution is state-regulated, so his work was not transferable. He had to start all over again. How fortunate could I be to be married to a man like him? Karl was always making sure I was okay, had everything I needed. He would do all of this without being resentful. Fortunately, the move to Indianapolis turned out to be good for Karl's career.

Karl was able to get back to the wine business. He made a good living out of it, along with additional benefits. It was a nice job. He was able to travel around the world to different vineyards and places and was doing well.

About five years ago, at the time of this writing, some of his customers, knowing his work, invited him to be a partner to restore and rebuild an abandoned Catholic church built in 1871 and turn it into a brewery and restaurant. He said yes in a heartbeat. He opened the restaurant as the managing partner and worked until he retired in 2018. This was a wonderful way for him to finish his career, an opportunity for him to leave a legacy. He remains a partner, just not the managing partner. It proved to be a legacy for him in terms of his career.

Conclusion

It all worked well. Everything was finally falling in place. Looking back, I feel that leaving Miami for Indianapolis was an excellent move. Earlier I talked about the TV show where the crew from the A&E network filmed my second transplant and recovery. At the end, I was reflecting:

"why me… Why have I been so fortunate to have my life saved twice? My life must be meant for something."

My move to Indianapolis enabled me to do some work to help other transplant recipients, mostly how to maximize recovery to get the most out of life during transplant and be prepared for what comes after the transplant. This was really what I feel like I was meant to do with my life.

I had two goals, the first one; I had been working on a standardized assessment, The Role Checklist Version 3[8] to measure how people are progressing toward returning to role participation after liver transplant and other major life activities. Now the assessment and administration manual are published. Nevertheless, I will continue to work with my international colleagues. I am traveling to Morocco in March, and at the time of this writing, I have been invited to present my research at a university in Rabat, Morocco. So, I'll be doing that. I am continuing to move forward with my plans, and there is no stopping unless it is for Karl and me to enjoy and appreciate traveling.

After I finish this book, my next big goal is to put all of the information that I know and have learned over the years about liver transplant recovery into a patient resource manual. Up to this point, my research has been published in medical research journals and presented at conferences and seminars for both professionals and transplant audiences.

---

[8] http://uic.flintbox.com

For this information to be helpful, it needs to be available to transplant recipients and transplant teams. I want to put it in a manual for transplant recipients so that they do not have to go through the uncertainty that I went through. May no one be put in that situation; I do not want anyone to suffer as I did. If someone does go through this, though, I want them to have a clear picture of what happens before, during, and after the transplant. Most importantly, organ transplantation is a serious business. I have met very few people through it unscathed, although most do not have the wild ride I did. It just takes a lot of courage to stay patient and stand strong, but believe me, in the end, you become unbreakable. This is the moment of realization that everything sure happens for a reason. This is a lesson for anyone dealing with a liver transplant, another transplant, major medical problems, or any of life's challenges. Hold on to your dreams; do not let your problems define you and hang in there.

Chapter 13
Giving Back and Moving Forward

Whatever the mind of man can conceive and believe, it can achieve.

-Napoleon Hill

It's not the place you are born that has an impact on your life; it's how you spend most of your time that decides the direction of your life. For me, I have spent many precious years of my life in hospitals and with patients, but today, I can honestly say that I do not regret any of it. I had never expected that I would spend nearly as much time as a patient as I did earlier as a clinician. But nobody knows what's written in their fate either. I experienced much pain and many emotions throughout it all, but at the end of the day, I learned! Karl and I unknowingly became a part of a huge community. A community we were able to give back to. The hospital became my second home. Fellow transplant candidates and recipients became my family. The cadre of medical professionals were our teachers and our overseers.

When I got my first liver transplant, I had no idea I was going to become a part of a larger group of people, a community that has been important support throughout my journey.

Giving Back to the Community

This community that we became a part of was powerful in our lives. And, we decided we would serve it in every possible way. Whenever we got a call for assistance, we never hesitated to say, *"Yes."* Moreover, after all, that Karl and I had experienced and learned together, keeping all the information to ourselves would have been an injustice. Mostly, we did not want more people to go through the frustration of the unknown that we had been through. We chose to make it our mission to give back to this community.

Post-Transplant Support Group

Before the first transplant, we attended a support group to prepare ourselves mentally. After the first transplant, Karl and I both became part of the outpatient support group for post-transplant recipients. This group met once a month, and it was loosely connected with the hospital and to the Transplant Foundation of South Florida as well.

The Transplant Foundation.

The mission of the Transplant Foundation was to support research, provide pre-and post-transplant education, and provide patient support during the transplant. I learned a lot from those sessions. During one of those sessions, I met Karen Cochran. She was such a brave woman, and it amazed me that she was a double lung transplant recipient. I was a rookie back then, and new to the transplant community, and I used to pay close attention to whatever this woman said.

It was April 1997, Karen talked about searching online, which was a concept most people did not understand at the time. Nevertheless, I knew a bit about it because I was working in academia, but still, even in academia at that time, our librarians did most of our literature searches for us. I saw Karen as an inspiration, so I went up, talked to her, and eventually, we became friends. Karen is one of those rare people that I continually admire in terms of how she has dealt with her transplant over the years.

Nonetheless, the time has its ways of turning things around – at the time, I had no idea I would eventually become the person in the transplant foundation who was in charge of the educational session. Every year, the educational sessions drew about 250 to 300 people who had some relationship to transplantation. They were either waiting for a transplant, had a family member who was waiting for one, or were transplant recipients, with their caregivers and families.

These sessions used to be full-day classes, and medical professionals would also join in. The physicians would come to share medical knowledge and discuss cutting-edge updates in the field of transplantation. However, the discussion was not always about transplants. Sometimes it would revolve around keeping people waiting for a transplant alive, such as ventricular assist devices, or the treatment of organ rejection. The topic varied every time, but there would usually be one physician who was either a kidney or liver specialist and another one who was a heart or lung specialist. There was much one could learn from these sessions, and the speakers gave of their time. I was proud to be instrumental in the provision of such quality information and spreading awareness.

The patient panel

One of the main features of these conferences was the patient panel. It was my specific responsibility to invite the speakers and moderate the panel. I enjoyed finding people who had been through the storm and stood strong at its face. It was important for me to find people who represented different stages in the process of organ transplantation and represented different types of organ failure leading to a transplant. I also sought out the family of donors. Therefore, while arranging these panels, I came across many different people with inspiring and heart-wrenching stories.

There was a panelist who really stuck out in my mind; a woman who donated her kidney to her daughter. I will call them Jenny and Carie. I met Jenny before my transplant as she worked at Florida International University. Her daughter Carie had been on dialysis for a long time, and finally, she was on the transplant list. The doctors approached Carie about the idea of family donation, and her mother, Jenny, met the criteria. If I recall correctly, Carie was probably starting college back then. Unfortunately, once she had the kidney and without the constraints of dialysis, she became careless. She felt as though her mother's kidney was enough for her and would just work perfectly fine. She thought she did not have to worry about taking the anti-rejection medication, and sadly, that was not the case.

One reason she avoided medications is that post-transplant medications cause swelling and resultant weight gain, both of which are not easy for a young woman in college. That said, Carie stopped taking her anti-rejection medications, and her body rejected the organ, which resulted in the kidney's loss. Well, her mother was understandably furious with her. The transplant team was furious with her, and truth be told, the girl herself was not very happy with what she had done.

Carie and Jenny were my guests on the panel and talked about their experiences. Jenny shared how she felt about giving her daughter a kidney and how she was overprotective at first *but ultimately allowed Carie to go back to college.* Carie told everyone that we had to realize that it was stupid to think that transplant recipients do not have to take their medicines once the procedure is done. Carie spoke about her lack of judgment and regret, mostly about what she had done to the gift her mother gave her – a gift that could never be regained. It was a powerful presentation and a revelation for some people who were transplant recipients. Following the panel, the mother and daughter thanked me for the opportunity. For them, it was important to be sharing the tragedy that had taken place due to carelessness so that others could learn and not repeat this mistake.

Karl was present in the sessions, and he spoke of the role of a husband as a caregiver during illness and surgery. He shared his personal experiences and spoke about dealing with a situation where your partner is getting a transplant. He narrated our story and shared his first-hand experience with everyone.

Many people related to the issues addressed by the panelists. Many hands came up with questions and reactions. As someone spoke, others listened and waited for their turns to share what they had to. This give-and-take among the members felt wonderful to those on the panel who chose to share their lives.

The caregiver panel was one of the big hits of the Transplant Education Forum. Hence, it was something that I always looked forward to, and I think I organized this forum for nine years before leaving Florida and coming up to Indiana. The Transplant Foundation of South Florida was fairly unique; most locations and communities across the country lack that kind of incredible support.

The Holiday Party

Another event that the Foundation organized in support of recipients was an annual holiday party. These parties would have around 3-5 hundred people, I may be exaggerating; this is my recollection, including transplant recipients and their families. The transplant team members would also attend. Hence, these parties made for huge gatherings where several hundreds of people stood united because of one thing they had in common – transplantation.

One part of the ceremony was the trimming of the tree. Every recipient would bring an ornament to honor their donor. At the appointed time, all recipients would surround the tree to celebrate the person who gave them a new life by donating their organ. There was not a dry eye in the room. The musician would always play an emotionally relevant song like, *'We Shall Overcome,'* and the song Celebration always followed this song. It was always a moving moment for all the attendees.

After both my transplants, I tried to contact my donor's family to thank them, but I never got a response. This is how it works: only the transplant coordinator knows who the donor is, and they are in contact with that person. Recipients can write a letter and give it to the coordinator, who then gives it to the family. The family can then choose to respond or not. Therefore, it's very much up to the family member to respond unless the coordinator believes that it's not a good idea. After all, it's not necessarily easy for a family who just lost a member to interact with the individual who received the deceased's organ.

I respect the right of the donor's family not to respond. It's entirely their choice. I still wrote to my donor's family several times just to let them know that I was doing well and that I appreciate their gift of the organ at the difficult time of their family member's death. I stopped after trying a few times, assuming they wanted to put the death of their loved one behind them. As has been mentioned before, I never heard back from them, which was okay, but I really wish I did. It would mean the world to me to just say *"Thank you."*

Being on the Board of Transplant Foundations

After working with the Transplant Foundation for about six years, I was invited to sit on the Executive Board of the Transplant Foundation and oversee their research initiative. They needed a procedure to evaluate research grants sent in by different transplant community members, medical staff, and other people who wanted to do research. I served in that capacity until I left South Florida in 2007 to move to Indianapolis.

The people on the Board of the Transplant Foundation represent various segments of society, fully engaged in supporting and promoting organ donation and transplantation. Eli Compton, the executive Director, became a good friend of mine. She is the mother of Erik Compton, who, as a child, received a heart transplant, and became an excellent golfer. He played in the PGA until he needed a second heart transplant, and then rejoined the tour before retiring. His entire family supports transplantation and are the epitome of people who live life to the fullest.

Those involved in the transplant community are healthy and engaged in promoting transplantation while raising funds for people in need of transplantation. I know of individuals admitted to hospitals for months whose families could not afford parking in the hospital's paid parking area. The Foundation was responsible for taking care of the needs of such people. Those are the kinds of things the Foundation will do regularly; aside from supporting research and education, they would give cash gifts to support the needy transplant recipients and their families.

I got involved in the transplant foundation soon after my transplant, as well as participating in several events that were organized by the hospital to celebrate transplantation. I remember the first time, maybe two years after my first transplant, I was asked to address the recipients and medical staff at the hospital. It was an honor for me, and I prepared carefully. I was well aware of what I was going to talk about in terms of receiving a liver and being given another chance at life. I knew it was going to be an emotional speech.

I wanted to keep my act together and get through it because this was a group that did not need an idiot jabbering about whatever while standing up there at the podium. I wanted to express my gratitude for these people who had been keeping me alive and had taken care of me. They deserved an authentic address, and I barely made it through, but I did. It was tough. There were several instances when I had to stop taking a sip of water or take a deep breath, and then just move on because it was not easy to get through it. It was tougher than I had imagined.

Training for Transplant Ambassadors

Another program the hospital and Foundation co-sponsored was what they called transplant ambassadors. A call was made for training as a transplant ambassador, but I could not accept the call because it was right after I had the stroke. I was pretty sick. However, Karl did attend. Later he participated in as many as ten different events and gave presentations as the caregiver of a transplant recipient. When the OPO, which is the Organ Procurement Organization, would go out and talk about organ donation, he would go and represent the recipients. That was the purpose of the transplant ambassador program.

Transplant Mentor Training

A couple of years later, a group out of California affiliated with the American Liver Foundation conducted a transplant mentor training. Such training programs were usual for us now, and Karl and I took part. The transplant mentor training is when we learn how to be supportive of people waiting for transplant or people who are just getting out of transplant and really need someone to give them support. It must be somebody who's been there and is well trained and organized. Hence, Karl and I both were called on at various times to talk to people. I was asked to replicate that training at Jackson Memorial Hospital twice, about two years later. I did it again about five or six years later at Johns Hopkins in Baltimore.

Those are only two of the organizations that we got involved in, in terms of giving back, but I think that direct or indirect involvement in these organizations not only supported our engagement with the idea of transplantation and normalized transplantation for us, but it also made us members of this larger community. We have many friends from that time. Unfortunately, there are way too many people from that group who have passed away since then because of complications arising from a transplant or cancers.

As discussed in previous chapters, cancers are more common in individuals who get transplants because they are immunosuppressed. This condition is called post-transplant lymphoproliferative disease (PTLD). It was tough. It is also the reason I needed a second transplant. They had to take me off all my immunosuppression so that I could survive the chemotherapy.

Karl talks about the class of '98, which is when I received my first transplant. There was a group of people who got their transplants at the same time. Following surgery, the doctors want you up and moving as quickly as possible because getting up and being active after surgery is shown to be beneficial for recovery. So, I was told to stay as active as possible.

It was quite interesting to recover among a number of people on the same boat as I was. We would walk around on the 15th floor of Jackson Memorial Hospital, which was the transplant unit. Everyone walking around the floor with an IV pole was a transplant recipient. We would often comment about each other's health. We would look at someone and say, *"Hey,* you're moving *pretty quick today."* Or things like *"Are you okay? You are slowing down."* We all became a family in a way that we got to know each other based on having gone through the same thing. These friendships made it a little easier to survive those days.

At the time of my transplant, there was a deceased donor who gave two kidneys and one liver to three young men between the ages of 25 and 30. It did not take these young men too long to figure out that they all had the same donor.

We do not get a lot of information about our donors, but we do get a little bit of information, which usually includes their gender, age, and how they passed away. Jack was the ringleader, and he was quite a character. He joined all the pieces of the puzzle and was determined to track down the donor family. He checked out all the newspapers, contacted a few people, and it did not take too long until he had a clue. It was easy to find the donor mom for these three guys, and they forged a wonderful relationship. These were the kind of heartwarming events you get to witness in a transplant unit.

The Transplant Games

The most fun of all our post-transplant activities were the transplant games. The transplant games are Olympic style games designed for transplant recipients. At the time, to qualify for participation, you need to have had a solid organ transplant, which can be of any kind. You also have to be six months past the surgery and have to have a doctor's clearance and all the other documentation needed. In the past few years, they have expanded the criteria and now allow bone, skin, and eye transplants as well. Anyone who received a transplant at least six months before the games would be eligible to participate, and believe me, it was so much fun.

Finding things that can divert our minds from our situation or give us some peace is essential, and I always looked for something similar to that. No matter what I decided to do, my husband was always ready to take that walk with me. In the quest to divert my brain, we both became active participants in the Transplant Games, Team Florida. I competed with Team Florida at the 2000 games in Orlando, Florida. We also went to Minneapolis, Minnesota, in 2004, Madison Wisconsin, in 2008 and Grand Rapids, Michigan, in 2010. Except for the first games when I was limited to bowling, I competed in swimming competitions, and I was a top medal winner for my events. Karl became an official team photographer for the games.

The Opening Ceremony

As I said, these are Olympic style games, so there is always an opening ceremony. In this ceremony, the participants march into the stadium by State. Of course, at different times, I was I with two teams, first with Team Florida, and then later with Team Indiana. The most emotional time of the whole procession is when the donor's families come in. They always proceed in last, and they come holding pictures of their loved ones who died and donated the organ. They also have balloons for the donor; it is such a heart-melting sight. We all had our team uniforms, which was when I really wished that I knew my donor family. One could not find a single dry eye in the stadium when this happened. These events take place at the football stadium, and there are a lot of people present, almost close to 10,000 people, including families, participants, donor families, and everybody else.

My First Games

The first time I participated in the transplant games was in the year 2000, and it was in Orlando, Florida. I participated in was bowling. Though I am not a good bowler, it was the only thing I could physically undertake. I had drains and tubes with bile coming out and everything else going on with my body, but I kind of packed them all up. I did terribly at bowling, but I was glad that I at least participated because I had a wonderful time.

After finishing my game, I went and watched Karen Cochrane swim, who I talked about earlier. This was for two reasons. One, I saw her as an inspiration, and two, I knew as soon as I got healthier, swimming is what I would want to do at the games. I have mentioned how much I love to swim. I went over to the pool and spent a lot of time watching the swimming.

Six people would be swimming at the same time in probably the 50-yard stroke, and after five finished, the last person was the one who people cheered for the most. It was a young man who was really struggling to get to the finishing line. Every single person present in the stadium was cheering for him, and it was an amazing feeling. The support is for anybody pushing hard enough to want to participate, and this guy was really pushing hard. Finally, he made it to the finishing line, and every one, on their feet, applauded.

My First Gold Medal

I had an amazing group of colleagues from Florida International University, where I taught Occupational Therapy. Sue D'Agati, friend and colleague, and her husband

Dean, both swimmers, helped me prepare for the transplant games by introducing me to Masters Swimming.

Though I did not win anything bowling in 2000, in the second game I attended, I won two or three medals in swimming. This would become my sport. I would win two or three bronze or silver medals every time the games were held. But the Gold was elusive.

The last games that I participated in were in Madison, Wisconsin. I'll never forget this because it was when I won my first gold medal, which was important to me. I kept getting silver and bronze medals, but I never had a gold medal. Well, here it was, I finally had my first gold medal in Madison, Wisconsin. I almost had a second one but lost it because of my inability to count laps.

Let me explain. I trained in a 50-meter pool, and the competition pool was a 25-yards. Therefore, I had to count my laps carefully. I believe I was doing a 100-yard breaststroke when I counted one, two, three, four, and so on to myself to measure the distance. When I finished and looked up, the clock was still ticking, and I said, "*What's the matter? It's over.*" The referee said, "*No!*" He goes, "*I thought you were resting."* It turned out I was counting wrong. I only swam six laps instead of eight.

Though I regretted it at first, everything turned out as it should. One of the women I was swimming with, in the same age group, was a frequent competitor of mine. She came up and said, *"Think of it as paying forward. You have so many medals, and so do I, but somebody else got a medal today who would not have gotten a medal if you had been able to count to eight."*

Her words amazed me and gave me a good feeling about the event. I made somebody else happy by not winning, and she was right, I did not need that medal. I felt much better about it. Earlier I felt foolish for not counting right, but what did I have to lose? I have quite a set of medals at home. There are many pictures of me holding up the medals in my team shirts, which is enough to make me proud. For me, the games were about camaraderie – although it is nice to walk around with multiple medals around my neck.

I had my gold medal framed, and it is on the wall of my transplant surgeon Dr. Andreas Tzakis.

The Coffeehouse

There's another event that takes place at the transplant games called the coffee house. In the coffeehouse, there are a bunch of people sitting together to talk and listen. Anyone who has something to say can go up to a podium and just talk for a while. I think there is a time limit of 10 minutes so that everyone gets an opportunity to go up and speak their heart. It does not necessarily have to be 10 minutes long; they let the discussion go on as long as it's worthwhile, then the next person goes up.

The coffeehouse audience is primarily families of the donors and people who are waiting for a transplant. One time, I felt that I had something to say. I went up to the podium and spoke my heart out. I said that I just want to thank donor families for donating organs, and I want to express how thankful I am for being able to get back my health. I said, "It's amazing how I am actually winning medals, when not too long ago, I did not think that I was going to survive."

It was a very spontaneous act on my part, and it took courage to go up there and speak. It was one of the things that I have done that just really makes me feel good.

Afterward, there were a lot of heartfelt comments, and it was so hard to listen to each one of them, people even came up afterward to me and said things like, "*My daughter is in the hospital. She's been waiting for a transplant, and she may not make it longer. I do not know what else to do. Please suggest what can I do?*"

I just felt so helpless at the time because of the inability to answer them, so I dealt with it through empathy; after all, I had been there. I had been in their shoes and knew how frustrating it was to wait for transplants because so many people were desperately waiting for donors. There is a shortage of available organs, and it's not easy to find a match. At the time of this writing, there are 114,000 people currently waiting for organ transplants, and a name is added every 10 minutes. On average, 20 people die every day, waiting for an organ transplant.[9] I am truly aware of how lucky I am to have had two transplants in a world where there are people out there who do not get to have an operation at all. This is the reason why I got involved in these activities in the first place. It was a form of 'giving back' for me.

---

[9] www.americantransplantfoundation.org

'Survive, then thrive.'

Once we were in Indianapolis, I learned how to disseminate my transplant research to support people who care about transplant support and education. I talked to Karl about wanting to set up an informational website that people could easily access and get all the information they need. I wanted this site to serve as a portal for people to share stories and raise awareness.

We established a transplant website called 'survive-then-thrive.com.' The website has been rolled into the larger website for this book. www.patriciajscott.com is now active, and all much of the knowledge that I possess will be available for people who are interested to learn virtually. Once I complete this book, as I mentioned earlier, my next agenda is to compile all the information from my research into a manual, a workbook, available to transplant programs, and to individuals interested in the process.

Both of these projects are very close to my heart because I believe it is part of giving back, and a part of recovery. It is like a brick over brick, creating a wall. Each piece builds on each other.

In terms of giving back, I am really proud to receive much recognition and two different awards for my research. One of the awards is from the American Transplant Association, and the other is the Bantz Petronio Award for Translational Research from Indiana University. To be recognized for doing research and helping people live better lives is really encouraging for me.

"Act as if what you do makes a difference. IT DOES."

-William James

Chapter 14
Life Now, As We Know It

I believe that I have mentioned this at least a million times, but I feel the need to say again that life is unpredictable. We never know what will happen, I keep repeating it because that is one thing people forget no matter how often it happens. If we are not vigilant, we are surprised when another curveball is thrown to us. We can never know what the next day would bring, so always try and live life to the fullest. Who knew we would one day be scared of conditions seemingly minor like fever and a stranger without a mask sneezing near you. Who knew these seemingly-minor illnesses would one day be declared as lethal? Today, when we hear someone has a fever or flu-type symptoms, we immediately begin to worry, wondering whether they are another victim of the pandemic disease.

COVID-19 has affected our lives in many ways. A lot of lives are already lost, and hospitals are filled with many struggling to survive. Everyone is drawn to the news and waiting for the moment they will escape the isolation, so they return to life as usual. Life started to return to an approximation of normal, and the cases rose. That is why I always emphasized on living life to the fullest. This pandemic has affected every aspect of our lives, and for many, their day to day lives suffer. Many individuals have become unemployed, businesses are facing the most significant losses in history, and many are devastated.

Entering COVID-19

It's June 19, 2020, or Juneteenth, and I am fortunate enough to be in my home in Indianapolis, complying with the stay-at-home restriction for the Covid-19 pandemic. I am anxiously awaiting to see when all this will resolve or if we will have to live with COVID-19 forever. This is a life changer for our society. People have found themselves new ways to live their lives as they are advised to stay at home, and if venturing outside, do so armed with a mask on and a hand sanitizer in the pocket.

I can relate to this situation because, back in 1998, after my first transplant, I was isolated as well. Medication has made progress since then, back in the 1990s, we were told to isolate ourselves post-surgery. We were advised to stay away from places that could contain germs, people with a cold, and children in general. I was cautioned about being highly immunosuppressed; therefore, I had to take special care of myself and my body. I had to stay out of crowds and avoid going to grocery stores or large gatherings where I may be exposed to someone with an infection or a cold virus.

It was easy at first for me to stay isolated, as I was in pain after the surgery. I was very happy to be sleeping all day. This was also making me weak and lazy. That said, Karl had made it his mission to take me on increasingly long walks to regain my strength. He even found new and interesting places to walk where I would not be exposed to many people. It was a nice experience. There were many gardens around our home in Miami, and this way, I was not locked at home, on the same bed, and in the same room all the time.

Nevertheless, I quickly became anxious and frustrated because of the same routine. I felt like the same day was repeating itself in a loop. There was a grocery store around the corner, but I was not allowed to go inside it.

I did become accustomed to isolation post-transplant, but it was for a short time. Perhaps that is why Karl and I seem to be able to adapt easily to the restrictions. This stay-at-home is surreal. However, it is similar to the one I had experienced after my transplant, except this one is happening not just to a few people or me, but to the whole society. Even in 2003, when I had my second transplant, the medication they used before surgery had less impact on my immune system, so I was under lesser restrictions at that time.

The Tour & Pandemic

The ban on all flights from Europe into the USA was announced on March 11, 2020. Karl and I left the USA on March 10. We were headed for a 15-day tour of 10 cities in Morocco, followed by a 7- day trip on our own in Portugal. On the day of the announcement, we spent the night in Lisbon, Portugal, with a 3:00 AM wake-up call to get to the airport for a 6:30 AM flight to Casablanca. It was 10:00 PM at home in the eastern time-zone.

I was in the shower when Karl saw news of the flight cancellations on his computer and turned on the TV. President Trump had announced a travel ban for all flights arriving in the USA from Europe. It was only later we were to find out that US citizens were exempt, and we would be allowed to return to our home country. At that point, we had few options left except to continue our trip. The airport in

Lisbon was a mess. The queues were incredibly long, and many people very anxious about getting back to their homes. Fortunately for us, we were flying Iberia Airlines to Morocco and already had our tickets, so we did not have to wait long.

The first few days of our Morocco tour were incredible. We were all attentive to the news. Our tour guide, Rasheed, was taking care of things as well. When he did not provide us with information about the magnificent country, he was on the phone, coordinating with other tour guides, and the parent company Gate 1.

Soon they called us back to Casablanca, and we spent five days waiting and looking for solutions. Members of our group would spend up to 12 hours a day in lines at the Casablanca Airport. The long lines at the airport, lack of masks, and no social distancing was convincing enough for me to stay away from traveling for a bit and work on solutions from our hotel.

Trust Your Instinct

I spent a long time reflecting on whether or not I should have gone. Once identified, I fell into the vulnerable categories, over 60. Being immunosuppressed placed me at high risk. Before I left, I had given a great deal of thought to this matter. Italy had a significant infection rate, and so did Iran. I was carefully following the news and following all the travel recommendations. There were no warnings or restrictions for Morocco nor Portugal.

I have talked before about how I feel about living my life. As it turns out, I could not find any errors in my decision-making. I started this book with a discussion of how I feel advice should impact our decisions:

"...understand where the advice is coming from, and it is usually out of care or worry. No one can know about your illness without either specializing in it or experiencing it first-hand. The advice may be helpful for some; however, it may not be healthy for you, but think about it. If you took everyone's advice, you would have your head spinning from continuous change."

And, most importantly:

"I discovered with time that success was related to trusting my inner self, though. Trusting your inner self

means understanding which advice to consider and which to edit out, and when felt appropriate, delete it. "

Reflection on my discussion about trusting my inner self means a fully informed inner-self. Facts need to supersede emotions and desires. Now that I understand the errors made by our President led to his delay of warnings, and the news that, if he had only announced one week, earlier that lives would have been saved, my decision would have differed. Given information about the virus and its prospective spread included facts, the risk, and the magnitude of the impending pandemic. I could have delayed the trip and saved myself and Karl, and our families, friends, and colleagues, a great deal of worry. Well, again, fate had other plans.

Fortunately, we returned home safely. I hope as many of us as possible make it through this public health crisis, way too many have already lost their lives. We returned on March 25, and by this time, our individual crisis being stranded in Morocco had become a population health crisis. At this point, I really wish to return to the safety of our former worlds. By the time this book is published, we will know much more about the situation changing each passing day, and hopefully, we will be able to reschedule our trips to Morocco and Portugal.

My advice? Stay smart and stay safe to honor those who devoted their lives to keep us safe. And most important*ly, know what will bring you happiness and live life to the fullest.*

NOTE to the reader

You will find the next two chapters different than the ones you have been reading. **Chapter 15** offers advice for people who find themselves entangled in the healthcare system, where no one ever taught them how to be a patient, and how to handle the role of a patient. I hope this will be useful for the many people who have said to me, *"If I only knew what to do… what I was in for."*

Those readers interested in liver disease progression from initial signs of failure to live with a liver transplant will find information in **Chapter 16**. Chapter 16 reviews the stages of transplantation as identified through my research, and it starts with Stage 1: 'Decline of Health' and continues through Stage 7, which is 'Return of Health.' The Stages are the same in the book as they are on the website[10]; the information is oriented differently, so you may want to read both.

I want to throw in a disclaimer. You will find some repetition here of stories shared in earlier chapters as they epitomize the event. Bear with me.

---

[10] www.patriciajscott.com

Part IV
Good to know before you start
Advice from experience and research

Chapter 15
Important and Productive roles: Enter the Role of a Patient

Being a patient was another unique experience for me. I realized that few people really know how to perform in the crucial role of a patient. It was not an easy lesson to learn, and that is why I decided to make it a part of this book. I do not want anyone else to be as clueless as I was of what they need to do in certain situations during this unavoidable journey.

At first, I was very demanding as a patient. After all, how do you really know how to be a patient? It is not something anyone can teach you. When asked what they wanted to be when they grew up saying, I have never met anyone who would say, *"I want to be a patient."* I can assure you I NEVER wanted to be a patient. The concept was foreign to me. With all the work that I have done with roles and identity, I know we learn things with time. We learn how to be a worker, as we get feedback, we have role models, and there are guidelines. The same is true of being a friend and a family member. We have learned these roles with experience. But how do you learn how to be a patient? The only information I have seen as readily available is patient rights. Patient rights are important however, they are not role expectations. Medical professionals are not trained to teach you how to be a patient, and certainly, there's no rulebook to determine this. It's something you have to figure out yourself; it is something I had to figure out myself. Today, I can say that I know how to perform well in the patient's role. I know when I need to assert myself and when to advocate for myself. I know when to speak, and I also know when to keep my mouth shut.

If I talk about being a patient, there are a lot of memories associated with it. My first memories of being a patient were in the 1960s when ice skating, I landed chin first on the ice while practicing a flying camel spin. There was blood everywhere. I recall the owner of the ice rink saying, "*No problem, nothing a few stitches will not fix.*" I was terrified. My father was called, and he drove me to Doctor Friedman's office, where I had eight stitches in my chin. For me, at age 14, it was a traumatic experience. However, my memories of the medical care I received was positive. I did not have any other medical situations for 15 years in the early 1980s. It was when I first identified that something was not right with me. These memories include concerned doctors who made me pay attention; the tremendous time commitment; and the ambiguity and inability to identify what was wrong.

I associate all of this with anxiety. Being a patient is an anxiety-producing experience. Many people delay or even refuse to go to the doctor due to this reason. Even though I experienced anxiety about my health, I could never have imagined anxiety was part of the reason I felt so off my game. This provoked the researcher inside me, and I set out to find out everything I could about this problem. I wanted to know what I needed to do to make it go away. I am sharing my experiences as a patient as part of this book, so anyone who reads it can learn from it.

When I researched the basic definition of a patient, this is what I found:

"Patient comes from the Latin "patiens," from "patior," to suffer or bear. In this language, the patient is truly passive – bearing whatever suffering is necessary and tolerating the interventions of the outside expert patiently. The active

patient is a contradiction in terms, and it is the assumption
underlying the passivity that is the most dangerous. The user
of services will remain passive in sickness, allowing the
healthcare professional to take the active part and tell the
user what to do. The passive patient will do what he or she
is told, and will then wait patiently to recover. The
healthcare professional is the healer, while the recipient of
healthcare services is healed, and does not take part in any
decision making or in any thinking about alternatives." [11]

When I ran across this definition, it made me think about my reference to considering my illness a contradiction. It connotes passivity and passivity as a patient is an unhelpful state. Truth be told, nothing about this description of a patient fits into my self-image. It all fits into the 'poor me' dependency. I was soon to find out this is how people expected me to behave. I did not. To explain my point of view better, I am going to use the Eight Principles of Patient-Centered Care to discuss my experiences of being a patient and how I learned to accept and reject the role.

---

[11] BMJ. 1999 June 26; 318(7200): 1756–1758.
doi: 10.1136/bmj.318.7200.1756

The Eight Principles of Patient-Centered Care

Researchers from Harvard Medical School developed seven of these principles on behalf of the Picker Institute and The Commonwealth Fund. The eighth principle is formulated by the Institute of Medicine, *"Crossing the Quality Chasm: A New Health System for the 21st Century."* Let us dive into the detail of each principle and how I connect them with my experiences as a patient.[12]

Respect for patients' values, preferences and expressed needs

Needs and Preferences

Before I explain this, I want to refer to something that happened while I was admitted to the hospital. At the risk of recounting the entire incident, after a procedure where I was sedated, I returned to the floor and was left with the bed rails up so I could not leave the bed. I understood these precautions as I just had sedation, and if I tried to get out of the bed, I could fall. Unfortunately, shortly after that, I vomited all over my face, hair, and the pillow. I rang the call

---

[12] The Eight Principles of Patient-Centered Care
https://www.oneviewhealthcare.com/the-eight-principles-of-patient-centered-care/

button for the nurse and explained what I needed. I then waited for what seemed to be an hour with vomit all over me. I called again and was very clear. *"I am still laying here covered in vomit,"* I said. The response was, *"We are still waiting for a call back from your doctor."*

There were many situations throughout my journey in which health professionals were very responsive to my needs, and in others, they were not. In the above scenario, I was totally dependent on the staff to help me. There was literally nothing I could do on my own. Therefore, to maintain my dignity, I asked if someone could come to help me without permission from the doctor. When a nursing assistant arrived in my room, she immediately realized my dilemma. However, the prior preference was to see if the doctor wanted to order something for nausea to avoid making two trips. Her actions reflected her desire to make only one trip down the hall instead of responding to my needs, but my current need was to clean up as soon as possible.

Expressing my fear

When I was receiving chemotherapy, I had a port placed in my chest that needed to be removed after the therapy was done. Because of my stroke's experience due to the misplacement of a central line, I was fearful of having the port removed.

I was familiar with all the attending physicians in Interventional Radiology as I was a regular patient, but at that time, none of the attending physicians were available. July is called 'amateur month' as all the new residents come in to start their placements. It was August. I explained my concerns to the new residents and said I would wait for one of the attendings. You should note that I was on a stretcher in the hallway, and two or three other patients were present. One of the transplant surgery fellows overheard this conversation and reassured me that he would stand by me. I trusted him, and he understood my concerns. I felt fortunate that I was not alone.

Important Advice to Patients # 1 – Do not beat about the bush. You need to be able to express your needs, preferences, and values clearly. This goes for every situation. If another patient's visitors are bothering you, the

TV is too loud, or if any other thing is causing you stress when you are trying to rest, speak about it and be clear in what you want. Even if it is our own family or friends who are bothering you, say it out loud. If you would like to have more company or less, speak up. You need to have the proper environment to heal.

Coordination and integration of care

Harvard University conducted research using the focus group method with patients and families who were recently discharged from a hospital. During this research, the focus group patients expressed feelings of vulnerability and powerlessness in the face of illness.

This takes me down the memory lane.

While I was in SICU (Surgical Intensive Care), the staff was visible and checked on me constantly. The day after my surgery, I was transferred to a double room on the transplant floor. In SICU, I was on IV pain medication, which could be dosed by pushing a button. When I was moved to the floor, my medication monitor had not been set up. I was in intense pain. This was during the shift change, and all the nurses were in a meeting. As I recall this story, I realize it sounds very selfish; however, I was scared and wondered what was going to happen to me. It was probably 15-20 minutes, yet it seemed like forever. I believe transfers from SICU occurred so regularly that for the staff, it was no big deal. Coordination to meet the patient's needs was not a priority. To me, this being my first surgery, it WAS a big deal. I was scared and in pain. The whole scenario made me feel like moving the patient (which was me) to free up the bed was their priority.

Important Advice to Patients # 2 – The need for continuous care for a patient is primary. For the health care system, not so much. Only I, as a patient, experienced the anxiety of the unknown. The unknown to me was the routine for the health care staff. When I was entering the unknown, I was not prepared. It is okay to be anxious, but it helps to know the constraints of the staff. It's really hard when you don't know them.

Information and education

Once, there was a time when I was shaking and freezing despite the temperature that day being 90-degrees. I have told this story before. Karl wrapped me in a blanket and drove me to Sylvester Cancer Center. It was two days after I had my second infusion of CHOP for a large B-cell non-Hodgkin's lymphoma in my spine. I remember it took three nurses to get an IV in me due to shivering, and Karl being kicked out of the room. A nurse practitioner at the foot of my bed, gave a long explanation of CHOP's side effects.

You all must be sure by now that I am an information junky. I want to know what is happening to me in as much detail as possible. In fact, my need for education once resulted in getting me fired as a patient. I never knew a patient could be fired. If you recall, one day, she told me, *"I cannot treat you any longer. I do not have the time to answer your questions."* I was effectively dumped.

Back to the story above, anyone who has been very sick knows it is not possible to process information with a fever as high as 104.7, and three nurses trying to insert an IV. The next morning, this same nurse practitioner came in to see how I was. I asked her to repeat the information from the night before, and she proceeded to do so and answered my questions patiently.

A short while later, I was walking down the hall with my mask on and my IV pole. When I got close to the nursing station, I overheard this NP complaining she had to repeat the information from the night before. She said, *"It makes me crazy when patients do not listen. Do not they know I have better things to do other than repeating myself?"* I was stunned to hear those words coming out of her mouth. I continued to walk down the hall. The next time she came into the room, I discussed patients' education and how it was well documented that hospitalized patients retain less than $1/3^{rd}$ of the information they receive while hospitalized. I also shed light on the need for written patient education materials, so they do not miss out on any important information. I did not need to mention the point about healthcare professionals gossiping about patient interactions. She got the point.

Interestingly, she did not mention that all my hair would fall out. It started that afternoon while I was in the shower. At the time, I had a lot of very thick curly hair, and I lost about $2/3^{rd}$ of it. I was embarrassed to leave a mess in the bathroom and rather horrified about my hair.

The cleaning lady came in, and I warned her beforehand about the mess to which she responded, *"I work on the cancer floor. I have no problem with hair, but thank you."*

Here we have two scenarios and how each scenario is different from another but still falls under the same category. Patients deserve to be treated with care, keeping in mind the sensitivity of their condition.

Important Advice to Patients # 3 – Educating yourself and having access to information is a principle here, but it is also your right. If you do not understand the medical jargon, ask for clarification. Never be afraid to seem dumb because certain information may seem very simple to a health professional but can be clear as mud to an average human being. Information, if it is very important, should be provided in written form. Hospitals are full of information that is unclear to the patients. Let me say that again…

Information, if it is very important, should be provided in written form.

My husband and I were in a situation where I was a health professional and not. Often, some information would go right over his head. There were occasions when I was asleep, still recovering from anesthesia, or had a high fever and was generally too sick; therefore, I would not be the one who talked with the physician. Later, I would grill Karl about the doctor's information, which was unfair as he was doing his best to understand it. He got to a point where he would say to the doctor or nurse, *"Slow down and speak clearly, please. English is my second language, and I have a hearing problem.* Both were true.

It is your right and your obligation to understand all the information. NEVER hold back from getting information that you need to manage your health. Remember, there are NO stupid questions, just stupid answers.

Physical comfort

My physical condition was not good in 2001. I had a tumor in my spine, which had fractured one of my vertebrae. The vertebrae are the 33 individual, interlocking bones that form the spinal column. It was identified by an orthopedist that I used to see for my back pain. There was a problem with diagnosing the type of tumor given its location inside the bone. The oncologist, Dr. Lebwohl, was working with Dr. Harrington, my hematologist, through a referral from my transplant surgeon and hepatologist. I was in a Thoracic-Lumbar-Spinal Orthotic or TLSO, to protect my spinal cord from the unstable fracture. I was in that contraption for nine months. Imagine having your spine held tightly together for months to avoid an injury to your spinal cord.

During this time, I was scheduled to present a paper at the World Occupational Therapy Congress in Stockholm. I was surviving through the regular use of Percocet. As I mentioned previously, by the time I left Sweden to return home, I was down to 1/2 of one Percocet because I was running out of medication. I was in severe pain.

Upon my return, I sent an email to all my physicians, describing my frustration with this persistent and unrelenting pain. Dr. Guy Neff, my hepatologist, was the one who responded. The level of the physical comfort of patients has a significant impact on their experience. Dr. Neff changed me from Percocet to Percodan, which was long-lasting and told me to take the Percocet for break-through pain.

Currently, opioid addiction is an epidemic in our society; much of it is attributed to the overprescribing of drugs for legitimate medical reasons. For this reason, the prescribing of medications for pain is under the spotlight. A friend and medical professional described an increase in the number of patients who are afraid to take opioids or any narcotics for pain. Over the past 30 years, I have found narcotic medications to provide welcome relief from pain. In fact, upon the occasion described when I had a spinal fracture caused by a tumor, I was taking tremendous amounts of painkillers. I needed them. When my pain subsided, I stopped. I let go of my medications without a problem when the pain was relieved. I also learned to follow the physician's advice as to the rate of withdrawal, especially if you have been taking them for a long time. I also know people who have become dependent. It is important to be aware of your potential dependencies and work carefully with your pain specialists.

Important Advice to Patients # 4 – If you are not comfortable, let the staff know. Understand that there are alternatives to pain. If you have a request, be specific. Instead of saying, *"my back hurts"* (which it will if you are in the hospital bed long enough), ask if they can recommend something for a sore back. Even better if you simply just say, "Can I have a hot pack? My back is very sore." No one should lie in a hospital in pain, freezing, thirsty, or needing to use the bathroom. I can tell you; nurses are busy people and often need to minimize multiple trips, so they will want to know your request over the intercom speaker. If you have a personal request to make, you can simply say, "I have a personal request." If it is urgent, just say urgently. And most importantly, if you need to use the bathroom, call as soon as the urge comes to mind.

Emotional support and alleviation of fear and anxiety

I assumed it was not the role of health providers to alleviate fear and anxiety but to be kind, with a caring attitude towards the patient. There were many occasions where health providers were cold and uncaring, and I was treated like an object. However, and fortunately, I also have many memories when health providers did provide the emotional support I needed on many occasions.

Cryptogenic Organizing Pneumonia

During my 2017 hospitalization for cryptogenic organizing pneumonia, one of these situations occurred when I needed and received alleviation of fear and anxiety the most.

I was in the hospital. When Karl left that night, we said our goodbyes. It was an emotional experience, and then fear took over me. I had no reason to believe that I would make it through the night. My breathing was getting more and more difficult with every passing minute. I had been on pressurized oxygen for over a week. It was apparent the doctors were out of options. None of the viral, bacterial, or fungal cultures produced any information.

Later, Dr. Audrey Krause, the psychologist from the transplant unit, a professional colleague, and also consider a friend, came by. I told her about my fear that I would not make it through the night. She stood, hands crossed behind her back, leaning against the wall at the foot of my bed. Her professional and caring responses to my concerns welcomed me to continue expressing my fears. Her demeanor reassured me it was okay just to talk. She did not tell me my fears were unfounded and baseless; instead, she showed me respect and care. Talk about someone who has her roles straight. At that time, she knew I needed her to be a professional psychologist and, at other times, a friend. Talking to someone and getting acceptance instead of placating me helped me get over my fears. Which was good; it also helped with my breathing.

Relisted for a Transplant

There was another time I can remember when I was very sick and was relisted for a transplant. I was yet again admitted to the hospital. It was the middle of the night. I rarely slept well in the hospital, and this night was no exception. I was drifting on and off when I caught myself thinking I could just relax and let go. I, for once, thought that not fighting to live would be easy. I awoke startled and realized what was going on. I needed someone to talk to and rang my nurse's call button. One of the surgery fellows, Dr David Levi, was walking by and saw the light. He came in, and I told him what had happened. He sat with me until the sun rose, the day shift came on, and breakfast was ready. We talked about death and spent a lot of time talking about living and the future. He had a huge and generous spirit.

Round three of CHOP

I had been lying on the couch, listless, and shaking. Earlier that day, I was frustrated with myself for being so dependent and vowed to stop. Hence, I decided to go swimming. I mentioned this swimming incident before.

Later that day, when I was shaking and running a fever, Karl called Debbie Weppler, the Head Transplant Coordinator, and told her what was going on. Debbie had Karl bring me directly to the 15th floor, skipping waiting for the admitting department, and got me immediately inside a room. She came in to talk to us, and I told her about my frustration. She listened, and later that day, the psychologist came and spent time with me, discussing my frustration with being so sick and so dependent on Karl. The psychologist involved Karl in the conversation. After that, when my labs came back, I was placed in isolation. My resources to combat the chemotherapy were zero.

The humanity of health professionals is amazing. I do believe nurses would like to have the opportunity to spend more time with needy patients but are stretched by the staffing shortages.

These 3 three examples epitomize tough times for me and how the humanity of these health professionals made all the difference. It is important to be able to express your fears and ask for help. We cannot expect anyone to read our minds.

Important Advice to Patients # 5 – When you are worried about what will happen next, be direct. Start your statement with sentences like, "I am worried about..." or "I am concerned that..." They both are direct and to the point. That is what you need to do; to get the message across. However, "What could happen to me..." is not a direct statement. Do not ignore warning signs such as a fever. Especially if you are at home, ask for help. If you think you should not drive, then you should not. Share your fear and anxiety. If you need counseling- ask for it, you would hardly be the first person overwhelmed with everything that is going on.

Involvement of family and friends

Family and friends play a crucial role in your recovery. I am fortunate for I have a loving, committed husband, awesome family, and supportive friends. Unfortunately, I have experienced many 'roommate' situations where this proved not to be the case.

If patients are hospitalized, it is for a reason. They are sick. Cell phones are both blessings and curses in hospitals. On the one hand, people unwilling to turn off their phones are subject to being woken up from much-needed sleep. On the other hand, these cellphones provide important access to loved ones looking for updates and wanting to express much-needed support.

This principle recognizes the interests of the family in the patient's care. I remember one evening after my surgery, the transporter came to bring me down for an x-ray. In working on transferring me from the bed to the stretcher, I was in intense pain and needed a maximum assist transfer. They fumbled, and Karl was getting agitated. He finally said, *"Put her down. Come with me. I will show you where there are a dozen portable x-ray machines. Leave her in bed and bring the machine to her."*

He had to raise his voice. He should not have to do that. Karl was well-known on the floor and well-liked. He also had a reputation for not holding back if he felt my needs were not being met or taken care of.

Karl also felt he should have been included more in discussions about my treatment that was planned in the hospital. With my background as a health professional, I could understand everything easily, yet my attention and memory were not up to comprehending the information.

This is why Karl often felt uninformed and unprepared by a lack of inclusion.

One time, Karl was at home and received a call at about 10 PM; he was informed I had been moved from the transplant floor to ICU. They told him not to worry and that I was being taken care of. Of course, he was at the hospital immediately. He was walking into the ICU when one of the transplant surgeons was walking out. *"Have you seen Patty yet?" "No!"* He answered. You know the rest of this story from earlier in the book.

As my primary caregiver, and ONLY family within 500 miles of the hospital, Karl was alone in his role. He was an excellent caregiver, attendant to my needs, and not demanding of me. He protected me from too many visitors. He knew me and respected that when I was in the hospital, severely sick, I preferred to rest and heal. He also knew when I needed company. Therefore, it is important to have designated friends and family involved in the treatment.

Important Advice to Patients # 6 – Friends and family are critical to much-needed support when you are sick. They have the right to be listened to, but the right is limited to only as much private information as you decide to have shared. In the modern days of social media, it is important to inform your family and friends about your privacy choices. If you have the unfortunate friend or family situation where a certain individual tends to annoy or 'stress-out' you out tell the staff who will take care of it. If a friend or family member puts private information on social media, tell them to stop. Medical information belongs to you. Also, I recommend when a health provider explains something, and you are too sick or too tired to pay attention, just ask them to explain it to a family member present or call you later.

Continuity and transition

Patients and Caregivers often find it difficult to take care of themselves or their loved ones when they go home. Meeting their needs can be difficult in the beginning because it takes a while to get used to the transition from the hospital.

The first Transplant

After my first transplant, I went home after one week. It's really scary going home after a transplant because, in the hospital, they check your blood at least two to three times a day. They tell you what your lab values are and are always adjusting your progress with the amount of medicine. This is important in controlling your blood levels. Contrary to this, when you are discharged, you are all of a sudden by yourself entirely. Technically, I was not alone, I was with Karl, but he is not a nurse.

I had eighteen prescriptions that had to be taken at different times during the day. I was so sick of opening bottles and closing them back; it just made me crazy. You could tell that I was not thinking very well with what I am about to tell you. Out of frustration, I took a big glass bowl and poured all my pills out in it so that I could just pick them out when I needed them instead of opening all those bottles all over again.

I did not realize Karl was noticing me and said, *"What are you doing?"* I said, *"Well, I'm making it easier to get myself medications when I need them."* He said, "You better put them back in the bottles, right now!"

I felt like a little kid, but he was right, so I put my pills back in the bottles.

I realized later it's almost like a post-traumatic stress response because, in the hospital, your bloodwork is done daily if not more often, and they come back in about two hours and tell you your current condition. You learn to count on this information. It is reassuring. But when you are an outpatient, you go to the hospital or the lab, get your blood work done, and then you go back home. Sometimes you have to wait two or three days to find out the results.

It was stressful waiting for the results; I had anxiety attacks wondering what my blood reports said. I did not feel bad, so I never knew if I was okay or not. I now have access to the hospital's portal so that I do not have to go all the way to the hospital to get the results. Going back home is hard!

Important Advice to Patients # 7 – There is no need to panic. It will be difficult at first when you get discharged, but with the help and support of your family, you can get over anything. Just remember to go for regular checkups, coordinate and plan ongoing treatment and services with your specialist after the discharge. You will also be sent home with detailed information about medications, physical limitations, dietary needs, etc.

Access to Care

As I said earlier, patients can get anxiety attacks after getting discharged, knowing they are on their own, or with a family member or caregiver. That is why patients need to be sure that they can access care anytime when it is needed. Patients will need easy access to transportation, hospitals, clinics, physician offices, scheduling appointments, and clear instructions on when and how to get referrals. This is particularly a problem for people returning to rural communities. I lived close to the transplant center, and this was not an issue for me. However, I worked with many post-transplant patients who were returning to homes away from the transplant center with access only to small community hospitals. Before returning home, ask your coordinator to provide you a list of Dr's names.

Your medical records should be sent to your hometown physician. You should also have a copy of these records for emergency reasons. Have a plan for if you run a fever, experience, pain, and infection at the incision site and other problems that may arise. You will be sent home with a post-transplant manual. Make sure you read it before you leave and ask questions about anything that may be a problem for you and your living situation.

Important Advice to Patients #8 – Do not panic if you feel helpless. Be prepared. Make sure you have everything you need, even when you are back to a healthy lifestyle, you never know what is going to happen next. You need to have easy access to care when things go downhill.

These are the eight principles that you can use to understand what it means to be a patient. There is an enormous shift in health care to empowering patients to take an active role in their care plan. However, do not be surprised when you run into health providers who expect you to be passive patients, as in the definition I provided earlier. I urge you to accept when you are sick and need to be submissive, to be passive. I urge you to recognize when you need to start taking control of yourself, ask questions, be assertive, and manage your situation. There is new technology to help transform healthcare facilities and help organizations to engage with patients regularly, which will hopefully lead to tremendous and improved outcomes. It is high time that we all shed light on important yet highly ignored and even barely noticed struggles that patients have to go through and play our part in making it easier for them to survive.

"But.... responsibility for your health is on your shoulders!" me – PJS

Now that I have contextualized my experiences into the 8 Principles of Patient-Centered-Care into examples, there are a few more issues on the top of my mind about the battle of putting your role as a patient behind you.

Your disease is not your Identity

Believe me; no challenge is worth giving up your identity – and don't let it be stolen either. I have seen many living bodies with no life; once they became patients, they failed to escape the role for the rest of their lives. Remember the definition of a patient at the start of this chapter? Do not let that continue to be used any longer than necessary.

It's not just you, the patient, but also the people around who do not let you escape. Others will ask you and your family about your progress, and the conversation may turn to you as a disease instead of you as a person. During my research, I came across many such people, but two specific occasions stand out in my head.

Being a Transplant Recipient

I had moved to Indianapolis, and my second transplant was seven years behind me. One of these incidents happened with a very well-renowned hepatologist, Dr. Paul Kwo. He knew I was researching recovery, and he was very willing to involve his patients in my research. One summer, he came to me and asked me if I could help his son with an internship. His son was in high school and needed an internship because he eventually wanted to apply for a medical school.

He asked me if his son could be of any help, maybe he could file papers or organize things for me. I said, *"Sure, I'll work with him."* He then said, *"Okay, are you available today?"* He brought his son over to my office on the same afternoon, and I gave his son some reading material and said, *"These are the things that you need to know about liver transplant. These are the patients' experiences."* I did not give him technical research as he was a high school student.

I gave him some writings that could help him understand where people are coming from. As an example, I referenced one of my experiences during the transplant. The boy's father, the physician, and hepatologist looked at me and said, *"What? Are you a transplant recipient?"* I looked at him and said, *"Yes. I am."* At that point, I had known him for probably six or nine months, and he had no idea. I said to him, *"I just assumed that you knew."*

This same thing happened again when I was working on a study about people receiving combined kidney and pancreas transplants. One of the nephrologists, a kidney specialist, was part of the team. He was very interested and engaged in the research. This was also when my primary care physician was very much concerned about my kidney function. I said to him, *"Well, for somebody who's been on the transplant medications for 20 years now, I'm doing really well.* He said, *"I want you to see a nephrologist,"* And I was left with no choice but to agree. I said, *"I would like to see Dr. Tim Taber,"* and he said, "Okay."

I walked into my appointment without any document or any paper in my hand. Dr. Taber looked at me and said, *"What are you doing here?"* I said, *"Well, my primary care physician is concerned about my kidneys, so I am here for a checkup."* He said, *"I never knew you were a transplant recipient."* I thought to myself if I should carry around a tag that tells everyone I am a transplant recipient. I said, *"I am accustomed to it. I am aware a transplant recipient does not look any different than anyone else. However, I am a transplant recipient, and I am happy to talk to anybody about it anytime. But I guess people do not know that about me. It's funny, but it's such a huge part of me, I own it."* A lot of such incidents still surprise me.

I also had an appointment as an Adjunct Professor of Surgery to conduct my research. Sometimes, I'll start talking to the medical students there, and they asked questions in return. This way, when they would find out about my transplant, it would also hit them like a shock, *"What? You had a transplant?"* It gets people's attention and not always in a bad way. But this should not be the only thing you must be identified with. Your own identity should be separate from your disease.

I have to tell you I continued to work with both physicians handled the news very professionally. Paul Kwo became my hepatologist and a friend until he left to become head of Hepatology at Stanford. Tim Taber continues to treat me the same. If anything, I think his estimation of me increased.

It always amazes me how people get surprised when they see somebody who is healthy, living their normal life, and they just talk about it without any problem. They then say,

"Oh, wow! That's very impressive." I believe it's very impressive that somebody is not stuck when they have to constantly tell the world they had a transplant or any other disease.

I always compare such stories with the people who went to war. Even after twenty-five years, the only thing they have with them or they want to talk about is war. The same is the case with people that the only thing they want to talk about is their transplant, which can be annoying. Other people try to avoid such patients and run away from them because of their repetitiousness. When the same patients start living their normal lives and finally escape the role of a patient, they are surprised and appreciate it. I do appreciate it a lot.

I think a positive lifestyle also makes a good case for promoting organ donation. The best example you can set for motivating people for donation is by living a productive and fulfilling life after a transplant.

Patients are sympathy magnets

Each time I reveal my medical history or at least a part of it. I get the 'poor-me' look or a shocked, amazed look. I much prefer the latter to the former. In this world full of sympathy magnets, be self-reliant and stand strong. That is why I chose to define myself as a person who lives a normal life. It's my way of telling the world that such behavior is a cliché that I decided to go against. Unlike people who have carved their identity around survival of an illness. My advice for any of such people is, "*Just get over it, or soon people will get tired of you.*" They will also not take you as seriously with time. But it is much more than that. Now there is one important caveat here. Someone who overcomes an illness and dedicates their life in a positive and productive way, volunteering, promoting awareness, or fundraising, has found a way to channel their passion in a positive way. This is great!

Again, my background as an occupational therapist helps me to understand how there are people to whom their experience as patients is the most meaningful time they have ever had. Therefore, there is nothing else in their life that they feel good about. They do not have another identity. It is not dissimilar to a 'stay-at-home' mom, whose child(ren) has moved away, and it impacts her sense of herself. Re-conceptualizing primary roles and transitioning to new, satisfying, and productive roles is essential for a good quality of life. So, dear recipients or survivors of any other disease, look for a purpose! You cannot just sit and wait for the world to tell you who you are. You need to look for opportunities and get involved back in life. If you are struggling, run as fast as you can to your nearest occupational therapist. Start thinking about how you can be productive, keep your body active, and establish an identity outside of the hospital.

It's not that I have only seen victims. I am telling you to get over it because I have met so many wonderful people post-transplant who have really worked hard to regain their identity. I have also helped many people professionally to get past that identity of a transplant recipient because that may be exciting for somebody once, but after some time, you just want to move on. I mean, if you were not a transplant recipient, who would you be? For many people I have met, the answer lies in volunteering for a transplant or donor awareness organization.

I have learned a lot from my experience as a patient, occupational therapist, and researcher. Add to that Family member, Friend, and so on… I choose to live life fully and share my learning with anyone who will listen. I have been helping people heal back to their older self or to form a new identity separate from their disease. In contrast, the idea of writing this book came into my mind later. I am living my life the way I always wanted to, and I feel like I can contribute in better ways to the community I am a part of and give back to the world something larger than myself.

At the end of the day, I wish for every person who has had challenges not to let your difficulties define you. Remember that your identity should be so secure that when somebody walks away from you, they do not take you. Escape the prison, the patient's role creates inside your head, and finally, look to see the world from a new perspective. This will change your life completely, just believe!

"Two roads diverged in a wood and I – I took the one less traveled by, and that has made all the difference."

- ***Robert Frost***

Chapter 16
The Seven Stages of Liver Transplantation

I cannot believe we are at the end of this book, and if you are reading this last chapter, thank you for walking my journey with me. Writing this book was a roller coaster journey for sure, but writing gave me peace, knowing that I am giving back to the community that helped me become who I am today.

Chapter 16 is an informative one. It is about the seven stages of transplantation. These stages are determined by my personal research and my personal experience. Given my early frustrations finding information, I always wanted to give people access to what I discovered.

The Seven Stages

Here are the seven stages of a liver transplantation process experienced by most people. Before we hop on to the steps or stages, I would like to add a disclaimer here. As I said before, these stages have been developed based on research and personal experience; every transplant patient does not go through all of them in the same manner. You will gradually learn about each one of them and how your body responds throughout the stages.

The stages in this chapter are also published in the journal *'Occupational Therapy in Health Care.'*[13] They revolve around how, during transplantation, the psychological, physical, and physiological factors impact your emotional and cognitive functioning and how these factors interact with the attitudes of others. The research addressed many factors but mainly focused on:

- The impact of liver failure, and the waiting time on you and your relationships with your loved ones;

- Strategies to be pro-active and maintain emotional and physical strength such that you will experience fewer problems with the transplant process;

- Ways to maintain involvement in valued activities and roles; and

---

[13]Scott, PJ (2011) Occup Ther Health Care. 2011 Oct;25(4):240-56. doi: 10.3109/07380577.2011.600427. Epub 2011 August 9.

- finding a comfortable fit between the previously sick you – and the newly transplanted you.

Background

Every person that goes through a transplant experiences each Stage differently; many people go back and forth. It all depends on your physical health and the way you move through illness and health. For example, you can be listed for a liver transplant, and then be removed because the status of your disease and health continually changes. Some people experience fulminate liver failure, which means the liver fails quickly, and they start at Stage 5: The Transplant, before having time to prepare for it.

The process of waiting for, receiving, and recovering from a liver transplant can completely disrupt a person's life. I know a young woman who went into labor with twins and woke up 1500 miles away in a strange hospital with a liver transplant and no twins around as they were back at her home hospital. Imagine giving birth to twins and not even being able to have a glimpse of them? Imagine waking up and not knowing where you are and what exactly happened to you.

In my situation, I went through the early stages as predicted, got Stage 5, was ready for Stage 6, then my liver failed, so I went back to stage 3, quickly moved to Stage 4, and then waited in Stage 4 for six months.

People tend to fear transplantation, and I believe they fear it for the right reasons. I am writing this book to decrease this fear, because for me, the idea of what may happen made things less scary. I have known the fear of what's going to happen next. I have experienced the fear of whether I am going to survive or not. I have been through the fear of not understanding what doctors tried to tell me, and I have been through the fear of not knowing what's best for me. What is most important is to keep yourself as healthy as possible, so you are ready for whatever confronts you.

This motivated me to make this chapter a part of my book. I just hope that the information I share with you will help many people prepare and handle the challenges you may face during and post-transplant. I hope I can decrease the fear and anxiety for the people going through what I have survived.

Let us now discuss the seven stages of the liver transplantation journey.

Stage 1: Declining Health

In the first Stage, your health will begin to decline, but you will most likely remain unaware. The beginning of liver disease can be severe or subtle. It tends to come on quickly or gradually. The person affected may or may not have a diagnosis. Therefore, the idea of whether they are going to get a liver transplant immediately or much ahead in the future is most likely unknown.

So, in the first Stage if the arrival of the disease is severe, there will be very little or no time for the patient to stay on Stage one, and he or she will rapidly move onto the next Stage, which is organ failure. An average healthy person will not show symptoms immediately when entering this Stage. Performance problems are not usually seen unless individuals have a preexisting, debilitating condition, independent of liver disease.

What that individual does is look for a reason for their symptoms and become frustrated because they are unable to perform at a prior level. They also fail to discover what is wrong with their body which frustrates them even more. The symptoms of liver disease are not usually visible, and others, including their significant others, family members, friends, and co-workers, may perceive them as complainers or hypochondriacs. This is the initial Stage, so it may take time to discover what is actually wrong. This Stage was really annoying for me. I almost thought I would lose my mind. I was frustrated and irritated, not knowing there was a disease-causing my liver to deteriorate. That said, this Stage is often considered the easiest, but the mental pressure and fatigue people experience starts to mount.

Stage 2: Organ Failure

Then comes the next Stage, where things are about to get worse. In this Stage, the liver fails to remove toxins from the body, ultimately producing symptoms like increased fatigue, ascites, forgetfulness and confusion, depression or anxiety, and trouble falling asleep.

The Diagnosis

This Stage involves the authentic diagnosis of liver disease. The person may struggle to understand all the medical information they are bombarded with. During Stage

2, people close to the person experiencing a liver disease start to become more aware of the seriousness of their illness. The doctors may inform the patient that a transplant is a possibility so that they can prepare themselves. Needless to say, the news of a possible transplant is overwhelming, and reactions of denial or fear are common.

Critical Health Conditions

At this point, the health of the individual with a liver failure starts to deteriorate. The individual is unable to maintain the same levels of energy and concentration as before their liver started to fail. The demands of usual responsibilities start to exceed their abilities, as their physical and cognitive health start to decline.

The person with liver failure now has to balance the role of a patient with the performance of other roles and responsibilities. They have to be their old self and perform their former duties while taking on the new demanding patient role. At this Stage, the individual now experiences critical health conditions, which means they have to take care of themselves and pay extra attention to their body. The feeling of lowered competence and frustration experienced in Stage 1, increases at this point.

If we look at the best outcome, the treatment leads to remission or cure, and in the worst, it may lead to death. If transplantation is seen as the best and most ideal treatment, the person moves to Stage 3.

Discovery of My Liver Disease

I was working as the Director of Adjunctive Therapy at a psychiatric hospital in Oklahoma. The hospital conducted medical screenings as part of a wellness program. I was told I was very healthy and physically fit, yet I should follow up with my family doctor about my high liver enzymes.

After nearly two years of continuous testing and head-scratching, I was diagnosed with non-A non-B chronic active hepatitis, which over time, became known as Autoimmune Hepatitis. Over the next 15 years, I experienced repeated flare-ups and was treated with prednisone with tapering doses to reduce liver inflammation. In my case, it was a treatment, not a cure.

What is Autoimmune Hepatitis?

Autoimmune hepatitis is a chronic disease in which your body's immune system attacks the liver and causes inflammation, as a result, damages the liver. If not treated on time, it may get worse and lead to complications, such as cirrhosis.

Symptoms and causes

The most common symptoms of autoimmune hepatitis include poor appetite, feelings of tiredness, nausea, pain in your joints, jaundice, and pain over your liver. Some people show no symptoms at the time of diagnosis, but they may develop symptoms later. The causes of this disease are yet to be discovered.[14]

What diseases lead to transplantation?

A person needs a liver transplant when the liver is damaged beyond the body's capacity to repair it. Alcoholism and drug abuse are often associated with liver problems. Cirrhosis is associated with alcohol. In actuality there are

---

[14] Autoimmune Hepatitis
https://www.niddk.nih.gov/health-information/liver-disease/autoimmune-hepatitis

many common and rare conditions that may lead to liver failure and need for a liver transplant including Hepatitis C virus, Chronic Infection, Hepatitis B virus, Non-Alcoholic Fatty Liver Disease, or NASH, Primary Biliary Cirrhosis, and Primary Sclerosing Cholangitis, to name a few. More recent developments are reducing and even eliminating Hepatitis C. Hepatitis C was a leading cause of liver failure, although more recently Hepatitis C is declining and NASH, or Fatty Liver, is increasing.

Reasons for liver transplants among children

One common reason for liver transplantation in children is biliary atresia in which the bile ducts that transport the bile from the liver to the gall bladder and help in digestion are underdeveloped. Reconstructive surgery may be undertaken during the initial few months of life to correct this condition. However, some children go on to develop deep jaundice and, finally, liver failure.

Stage 3: Decreased Performance & Referral to Transplant Team

During the third Stage, individuals are sent to 'pre-transplant service' for extensive tests to determine if they are eligible for a transplant. The qualification protocol varies by facility. Nonetheless, all of them are focused on the need for the transplant, the likelihood of surviving the surgery, social and psychological 'fitness,' the likelihood of the person to responsibly take medication and care for the transplanted organ, and the ability to pay for medication and other essential needs, known as the 'pocketbook' test. It is a long involved process. After all, with limited organs, the transplant team has an obligation to be assured the person can survive the transplant surgery and care for the organ once they have received it.

Denial

Patients usually start to fear at this Stage about the seriousness of the disease and start asking questions. They may go through denial because they refuse to believe that their body is that impaired. They may fear and find it difficult to accept it as part of their world. Supportive others may also deny the seriousness of the situation.

Supportive others start to notice withdrawal and lack of social participation. This can create a gap in social participation as the person stops meeting others' expectations, which can result in conflicts. The frustration often increases with the inability to engage and lack of interest, where appointments, evaluations, and procedures, now consume a huge part of the individual's time.

Anxiety

Anxiety is common among transplant candidates, and understandable when going through such a lethal disease. This Stage can be a time of higher levels of anxiety as the individual and supportive others are torn between hope that the serious step of transplantation is not needed, and hope that transplantation holds a solution to their deteriorating physical condition. Attending the pre-transplant educational sessions becomes an essential event for the patient, where the team presents transplantation as a serious step. The obvious exception is fulminate liver failure where the person either has a short wait or goes directly to Stage 5, the transplant. If accepted as a transplant candidate, the person moves into Stage 4.

Stage 4: Pre-Transplant Waiting Period

The process of losing capacity and becoming reliant on others is complicated. Do not ignore or deny your limitations; work with your loved ones; they cannot always know the depth of your struggle.

The biggest challenge one faces during Stage 4 is the need to stay as healthy as possible. This is difficult as the individual loses muscle mass, becomes malnourished, and fights against water retention due to ascites. Even the simplest of tasks can become difficult for them to perform, like regular trips to the bathroom necessitated by encephalopathy medications.

What is ascites?

The definition of ascites is fluid buildup in the abdomen, but in my case, it was all over my body. I talked more about ascites in Chapter 5. Ascites made it difficult for me even to bend my knees and to do things such as sitting on the floor. Diet and exercise play a crucial role in such situations, as better physical health is associated with fewer problems and shorter post-surgical recovery. Individuals are encouraged to maintain a typical daily routine. Candidates are told to remain in constant contact with the transplant team and be ready to move if they do not already live within 4 hours of the facility if in case an organ becomes available. A transplant candidate's whole life revolves around one phone call, the notification that an organ is available.

Stress becomes inevitable

During Stage 4, both mental and physical capacities are compromised, and the person experiences feelings of being in 'limbo.' The candidate and his/her health become the center of attention in the family. There is nothing that remains normal about their lives anymore.

This is when stress starts to build up. There is a feeling of loss of control, both by the candidate and his or her loved ones. The situation seems to worsen with each passing day. Stress can exacerbate underlying disorders and preexisting interpersonal problems.

Depression, adjustment disorder, and anxiety are commonly seen among individuals waiting for a transplant. Others see the individual as someone in the 'sick' role, and the individual's fear of loss of competence and helplessness is now reinforced. People start to respond to them as someone who is unable to meet the basic demands of their life. The ability to perform basic daily activities is compromised due to increased fatigue, anxiety; quality of life gets poorer due to deteriorating health and often encephalopathy. Literature about this period addresses interpersonal strain and decreased role performance in basic activities of day to day life.

During this waiting time, the individual and supportive others start to reformulate their health and wellness image. Information about the transplant outcome and contact with others who have had transplants influence their beliefs about what their life will be post-transplant. This helps them prepare for it physically and mentally. Talking to someone always helps; the major reason I used to attend pre-transplant educational sessions.

Americans with Disabilities Act (ADA)

For people who are working, if the employer does not know about the transplant, it is important to disclose. The consequence of disclosing is to activate job protections available through the ADA. Importantly these protections are not available if someone gets fired for any reason, and pre-transplant many situations may arise. Disclosure can be private and to the Human Resources Person, although accommodations typically need to be coordinated through the immediate supervisor.

Disclosure does not require revealing a diagnosis, only disability-related limitations. Once you disclose, it is your choice to tell co-workers. They are likely see you struggling and knowledge of what you are going through may be helpful or not. Your HR Supervisor can work with you. The two biggest problems are fatigue and encephalopathy. Remember, you can get fired for cause if you do not activate ADA protections.

Stage 5: Transplantation & Immediate Post Transplant Surgical Recovery

Stage 5 is the acute phase of recovery, which generally lasts for three months. When they finally call a candidate for a transplant, the candidate cannot be sure if they will get an operation or a dry run. In case you're wondering what a dry run is, it occurs when an individual is either notified to come to the hospital as a back-up to another patient or may even be on their way to the operating room when the news arrives that the organ is not viable. When this happens, the individual returns to Stage 4. I know a woman who had 7 dry runs.

Stage 5: Surgical Transplant

The actual surgical transplant is the acutely stressful part of the process for the supportive others. The patient is unaware of the surgery. However, he or she becomes increasingly aware of the pain and the impact of a high dosage of drugs during the immediate post-surgical period. They see a hope to recover mixed with feelings of fear and helplessness. I recall thinking, *"Why did I let them do this to me?"* The individual is self-absorbed and under the influence of high levels of anti-rejection medications, which may cause altered mental states as well.

As individuals stabilize medically, the attention transitions to discharge, and the subsequent challenges of self-care management at home emerge. Ideally, after five to seven days of healing, sustaining, and receiving the required guidelines, the individual leaves the hospital. However, complications are not unusual after and major surgery and transplantation is clearly a major surgery. Here the stay may be extended to weeks or months as the outcome may be highly unpredictable. As I said earlier, with transplantation, you are never sure what will happen to your body next. You may sail through, or you may be back in the hospital.

It is important to have preparations made for the person to come home to a very clean and prepared home. If the patient was the home maintainer, bring in a helpful other, be it a friend, family member, or a paid service.

Post Transplantation

Transplant teams do not just leave the patient on their own; in fact, they monitor the organ recipients for the rest of their lives. The first three months are crucial, as it is when the patient is at a high risk of acute rejection and re-hospitalization. Stage 5 continues through these three months. Those three months are the first post-surgical benchmark in survival. Fortunately, this period's survival rate is good enough; 9.5 out of 10 transplant recipients make it past this point. The recipient is required to stay close to the transplant center during the initial weeks following surgery.

Since they are highly immunosuppressed, patients remain under close physical and laboratory monitoring with frequent visits to the transplant clinic. The recipients follow specific precautions to assist with physical healing and to avoid infections. The team's focus is on their body's physiological responses to the transplanted organ, with support and reassurance to recipients and their families.

Patients are central, and all other activities revolve around them. Everything is new, frightening, and exciting, as they hope for a possible return of health. They have been granted another chance to live. During this Stage, the patient needs a lot of time and patience to heal. The body will require it's time to adapt to the new organ. During this time, the patient starts to feel healthy, as the residual toxins left by the dysfunctional liver clear out.

Return to independence in Activities of Daily Living (ADL)

As I collected data for my research done on a series of patients recovering from transplantation, I discovered that the most needed and challenging part of it all is the ADL recovery. I got to know how to respond when asked questions like, *"When will I be able to" (fill in the blank---- ------)?* I asked many patients questions during my research, which helped me get my hands – on detailed insights.

Patients individually or through their transplant coordinators can track their progress on a questionnaire called the Occupational Self-Assessment-Daily Living Skills (OSA-DLS). I have been developing, testing, and revising a transplant recovery program as per the need and demand. This program will be available to transplant centers and individuals as of the beginning of 2021. The program will help transplant recipients and the people who support them, to work their way through the remainder of Stage 5 – and through the remaining Stages 6 and 7. Under this program, the recipient will be able to share their progress with others, which will help keep each recipient motivated to recover.

Stage 6: Functional Recovery

When the risks of acute rejection and medical complications decline, stage 6 begins; Recovery. This is when healing and stabilization have almost taken place. The individual starts to try their wings as a recipient and begins making sense of where their lives will go. They conceptualize their role as a recipient and consider leaving the patient's role behind to start living a normal, healthy life.

At this point, the physical signs of liver disease have been eliminated from the body, and the individual begins to feel healthy. Fear of possible complications may persist as the routines of medications and bloodwork continue to be dominant.

Complications of Stage 6

Though it is a stage of recovery, a transplant recipient is always at risk. The complications in Stage 6 include rejection, loss of graft, debilitation, and can be as severe as death. Any of these can delay recovery or result in a return to an earlier stage. Individuals with uncomplicated recoveries stay in this Stage for 6 to 15 months before moving into Stage 7.

Some recipients fail to adapt to some of the physical, physiological, psychological, emotional, social, or occupational challenges that occur during this process. They may never move forward and truly integrate the identity of a transplant recipient. Instead, they retain the 'patient' identity, feeling vulnerable about the integrity of their health and dependence on the healthcare system. When they fail to move on, their demands from the healthcare system and their support system increase. It harms the physical and emotional health of the individual.

Every transplantation stage has a different concern; however, my research always focused on returning the patient's valued roles. In Stage 5, the attention and focus are for the return of the Activities of Daily Living. Whereas, in Stage 6 and Stage 7, the interest and focus are on restoring the patient's normal day-to-day roles. Every Stage focuses on returning the patient's valued roles, which is that ostensibly every patient wishes to go back to their previous routine. When the patient can finally stop living as a 'patient' and live the life they've always envisioned for themselves.

Stage 7: Return of Health

Stage 7 is the final stage in which the health of a person finally returns. At this point, the individual starts to feel back in charge of their life and health, which is a critical step. The patient is under the transplant team's primary care, and medical issues are central to the survival of the patient. At this stage, the recipient is medically stable and confident enough to make well-informed decisions.

Being a recipient includes taking the responsibility of self-management, including having blood levels monitored, taking medication, and knowing when to contact the transplant team. During any health crisis, individuals go back and forth from a recipient's role to the role of a patient. Stage 7 occurs when the patient's role is no longer a primary one in the recipient's life. They will always have the responsibility to care for their organs by NEVER missing their medication and being vigilant of any concerns related to their health.

All the new habits and routines adopted to protect the transplanted organ become integrated into usual behaviors.

Unfortunately, some individuals are challenged to move to Stage 7 and continue to see themselves in the patient's role. Some of them never get to experience the return of health to live life to the fullest![15]

---

[15] 7 Stages of the Liver Transplant Process
http://patriciajscott.com/livertransplantation

A Reflection!

Reflecting upon things is something that I am doing a lot while writing this book. When I found out I was sick, and not the usual kind of sick, I had no idea this sickness was to last for the rest of my life in one form or another.

But there comes a time when you are weak and tired of every day's hassle. This is when you spend most of your time in bed. It is not dissimilar to the current stay-at-home, response to the COVID-19 pandemic. This is when you truly get the time to reflect. Reflecting has really helped me in many ways; it has given me a sense of humanity. When I think about the beauty of this world and people ready to lend me a helping hand, the medical professionals who dedicate their lives to save the lives of other human beings, I feel proud to be surrounded by such amazing people. I feel at peace, knowing that humanity and selflessness are still alive.

All the things I have been through have given me perspective on life. I live my life differently. I want to give back the amount of selflessness and care I received during my sickness. But this new respective also kind of scares me, will I be able to do it justice?

Then I tell myself that when I am not sick, there is nothing in this world that I cannot accomplish if I set my mind to it. I just have to make little adjustments along the way and live an intentional life. We always make compromises along the way, whether we are a transplant recipient or not. We adjust according to the situations we encounter. It's not that we keep living the same life since birth, and then we die, we all undergo a process of self-evaluation to make the most of our current life demands and opportunities. It is an absolute necessity.

I truly believe that life is a journey with its fair share of ups and downs. If we are given a specific path, we have to be prepared to face the consequences. Then at some point, the road leads us back to where we started, and that's when we choose another. We have important choices to make because we will always have multiple roads in front of us. You look at one, find out it is straight and narrow, and then see another one that leads to a beautiful beach or a garden. However, you cannot just stay at the beach or garden there forever any more than we can stand there forever, deciding which way to go. Life should never stop at one point, and you should always have the spirit to keep exploring new options.

I believe that there must be a particular reason why this road was chosen for me. I was lucky enough to receive two transplants, while others do not even get the chance to receive one. I was able to recover and escape the role of a patient when some people live in it for the rest of their lives. To me, this life is a privilege, and I need to treat it as such.

Therefore, I always encourage all kinds of patients, not just transplant recipients, to try and avoid living in a cage. Roadblocks are in our heads. Life is not something that should stop at a certain point in time; it must go on. You must get on to what you want to be, what you want to achieve, and then see the real you, not what remains from the patient's role. You may not have control over the twists and turns forced on you by your illness, but you will be seen for who you are. The alternative is the identity of a patient, and that will be with you for the rest of your life.

So, live to the fullest. Do not live life with regrets. Keep your heart open to all sorts of experiences. Remember everything that I shared in this book because I shared it with utmost love and care. I shared it because I want people to learn and benefit from my experiences. I want to preach to as many people as I can, and today, I am the happiest, for I have accomplished one way of giving back to the world. Thank you for holding on this long. I hope that after reading this book, you can go out and live! I hope, through this book, I was able to restore your belief in yourself. Life is too short to waste in regrets and insecurities. Always try to maintain a positive outlook on life and surround yourself with well-wishers who help you see the world through an optimistic lens. When you have the habit of looking at the bigger picture, a beautiful life will unfold before you, and little roadblocks will only make you stronger.

"Limitations live only in our minds. But if we use our imaginations, our possibilities become limitless."

-Jamie Paolinetti

Appendices
A-C

Appendix A

Timeline of Primary Role Connections During events 1997–2002

DATE	EVENT
April 1997	Defended dissertation: received PhD
September 1997	Returned to hometown to see father home on hospice
September 1997	Hepatic encephalopathic coma the day before my father's funeral
October 1997	Evaluation for liver transplant evaluation
November 1997	Married Karl S Mann
December 1997	Placed on transplant waiting list
February 1998	First Liver transplant*
April 1998	Surgery for resection of hepatic artery
July 1998	Placed on list for re-transplantation due to severe rejection
August 1998	Return to work part lime
Aug 98- March 2001	Monthly hospital admissions for dilatations of bile ducts, AKA my roto-rooter treatments
January 1999	Return to work full time
June 2000	First time at Transplant Games in Orlando (Team Florida)

RESILIENCE

September 2000	Bilateral brainstem CVA due to misplacement of Central Line
November 2000	Return to work alter stroke
June 2001	Completed 3 years of bile duct repairs
December 2001	Severe back pain Skiing with friends and Ice Skating with Family
March 2002	Put in TSLO for fracture of L4; suspicion of cancer
May 2002	Named to AOTA's Roster of Fellows
June 2002	Traveled to Stockholm, S weden, to present at WFOT
August 2002	Chemotherapy and radiation for spinal cancer
October 2002	Stopped Chemo early due to "potentially fatal toxic reaction" to CHOP.
January 2003	Returned to work following cancer treatment
January 2003	Liver biopsy revealed chronic rejection
March 2003	Placed on waiting list for second transplant
May 2003	Stopped working; too sick, waiting on availability of liver
August 2003	Second liver transplant *
January 2004	Returned to work part-time
May 2004	Returned to work full-time
May 2004	Surgery for incisional hernia repair
July 2004	Won 3 medals in Swimming at Transplant Games in Minneapolis (Team Florida)

August 2006	Traveled to Sydney Australia to Present at WFOT, spent extra time in New Zealand
August 2007	Moved to Indianapolis
October 2012	Received the American Liver Transplant Association Award for Applied Research
August 2010	Traveled to Santiago Chile to Present at WFOT, traveled to Argentina
June 2011	Traveled to Germany to spend time with Family
October 2013	Stockholm Sweden for the International Institute for the study of MOHO
June-July 2014	Traveled through Southern Europe, Lectured and consulted at Zurich Institute for Applied Sciences
October 2014	Hosted the International Institute for the study of MOHO at IUPUI
July 2016	Received Bantz Petronio Faculty Award for Liver transplant research -Indiana University TRIP Institute
November 2016	Service-learning trip to Belize with students
March 2017	Promotion to full Professor
December 2016	Cryptogenic Organizing Pneumonia
April 2017	Return to work after pneumonia
April 2017	Invited to sit as Acting Department Chair
October 2017	Santorini Greece
July 2018	Traveled to Cape Town South Africa to Present at WFOT,

May 2019	Lectured at University of Chieti-Pescara In Abruzzo Italy about RCv3 translation
May 2019	Professional leave for writing in Puglia Italy
July 2019	Retired as Professor Emeritus from IU Department of Occupational Therapy
March 10, 2020	Trip to Morocco and Portugal Invited lecture at University in Rabat. Which was cancelled due to COVID 19
March 25, 2020	Repatriated from Morocco 5 days after all flights to USA cancelled

Appendix B

For Caregivers:
Q & A with Patty's husband Karl

Q: Patty portrays you as quite the saint. Are you a saint?

K: I am not a saint. Anyone who knows me would tell you that. When Patty was sick, it was pretty hard and a difficult time for both of us, and I am just a loving husband that wanted his wife to get healthy and back to normal life again. Often she was sick and in pain and there was nothing I could do except to take care of what she needed.

Q: This is quite a story. How did you survive?

K: I survived by taking care of Patty and doing what I needed to do. I kept in touch with family and friends. I attended support groups with Patty. I also recall a situation where she did not feel like going and I went all by myself. When I needed a break and could get away, I would go out with Tony and Frank, my best friends. If I could be away from home knowing Patty would be OK, I would go play golf with my friend John. It was important to get away. We had a friend in Islamorada who had a house on the gulf side. Patty would stay in the house or sit on the deck, she enjoyed the ocean and the fresh air. After a while she went out on the boat with us.

The other thing I did was to maintain my professional contacts and network so that when the time was right I could resume my career.

Q: Patty describes several situations in which you were upset with the way things were handled. Can you describe one from your perspective?

K: A situation that was most upsetting was when the hospital called to tell me Patty was in ICU. She had a stroke. The stroke was caused by a doctor inserting a central line in the wrong place. I was walking through the door and the Doctor said to me, *"You need to know we do not expect much."* It was very heartless, the way he said it--- there was no human compassion in his message. Thankfully, I did receive compassion from a transplant coordinator who took me aside, had me sit down and then and took me to see Patty.

Q: What is your advice to other caregivers?

K: Make sure you have a cleaning lady!

Seriously though, they tell you to prepare your legal papers and everything, wills, put cars, bank accounts, and other important property in both names. We failed miserably. In the commotion of emotion we kind of like waved it aside and did not give it much attention. Do not do what we did. It's very important. We should do that all the time in normal life, to have a plan for the future. If one of us ends up alone, do not have things you wish you could do differently.

Q. Any last words of advice?

K: Be prepared to put yourself aside. In the hospital I became Mr. Scott, we were married, and Patty kept her last name for professional reasons, so my identity as Karl Mann became Karl Scott.

Also, when friends ask if they can help, say yes. I did so just to have people come over and be with Patty, so she could not be alone and I could go for necessary grocery shopping. And even more importantly, you will need a break.

So, if friends want to help, let them. But also protect your loved one from too much company. Just pay attention, know when your loved one is exhausted and ask them to leave— or just say, no company today.

Trust in the medical professionals while your loved one is in the hospital but it is your job to identify if they need professional care when they are at home.

Most of all hang in there. It's worth it.

Appendix C

SELECTED REFERENCES AND PRESENTATIONS ON LIVER

TRANSPLANT SURVIVAL AND THE RCV3

NAME: Scott, Patricia   J.

CONTACT: resilience.pjs@gmail.com

WEBSITE: www.patriciajscott.com

EDUCATION:

PhD Doctor of Philosophy. Specialization in Public Policy
 Analysis Florida International University, Miami Florida

MPH Masters in Public Health University of Oklahoma, Oklahoma
 City, OK

BS Bachelor of Science in Occupational Therapy University of New
 Hampshire, Durham, NH

ACADEMIC APPOINTMENTS:

Indiana University	Professor Emeritus	7/2019-present
Indiana University	Professor (2017) Department of Occupational Therapy	1989-2019
Indiana University	School of Medicine, Adjunct Associate Professor of Surgery	2010-present
Florida International University	Associate Professor and Chair (2002-2007) Department of Occupational Therapy	1989-2007
University of Oklahoma	Assistant Professor	1984-1989

LICENSURE AND CERTIFICATION:

State of Indiana License	# 31004554A

American Occupational Therapy Association Certification Board	# 306274

LIVER TRANSPLANTATION PUBLICATIONS AND PRESENTATIONS

Scott, P.J. (2018) Using the Model of Human Occupation to support translation of theory into practice: MOHO over time with practice examples from around the world. World Congress of Occupational Therapy. Cape town, South Africa, May, 2018

Meidert, U., Bonsaksen, T., & **Scott, P.J.** (2018) Measuring Participation according to the ICF with the Revised Role Checklist. Clinical Rehabilitation. Clinical Rehabilitation 32 (11),1530-1539

Scott, P.J. (2017). The Disconnect: Survival ≠ meaningful life: Recovery post-liver transplantation. 15th Interdisciplinary Conference on Communication, Medicine and Ethics Indiana University Purdue University Indianapolis (IUPUI), USA June 26-28

Scott, P.J. (2016). Addition of a Daily Living Scale to the Occupational Self-Assessment. COTEC – ENOTHE Congress, National University of Ireland, June 15-19

Scott, P.J. & Taylor, RR (2015) Measuring Recovery of BADL and IADL: The Expanded Occupational Self-Assessment. 4th International Institute for the Study of the Model of Human Occupation, October 23-24

Sheets, A, & **Scott, P.J.**, (2015) Facilitating Role Recovery of Persons following Liver Transplantation. Poster. 4th International Institute for the Study of the Model of Human Occupation, October 23-24

Sanders, C, Schnurr, L, Tannas, H, Yoh, Lindsay & **Scott, P.J.** (2015). "The Impact of Hepatic Encephalopathy on Occupational Performance" to the 4th International Institute for the Study of the Model of Human Occupation. October

Sanders, C, Schnurr, L, Tannas, H, Yoh, Lindsay & **Scott, P.J.** (2015) "The Impact of Hepatic Encephalopathy on Occupational Performance" Presented at the American Occupational Therapy Association Annual Conference. April 2015, Nashville TN .

Sanders, C, Schnurr, L, Tannas, H, Yoh, Lindsay & **Scott, P.J.** (2015) "The Impact of Hepatic Encephalopathy on Occupational Performance" Presented at the American Occupational Therapy Association Annual Conference. April 2015, Nashville TN .

Halle, J., LeMond K., Robinson, I., Sloss R. & **Scott, P.J.** (2014) Supporting Healthy Lifestyles of Liver Transplant Candidates and Recipients. American Occupational Therapy Association 94th Annual Conference and Expo April 3-6 Baltimore MD

Scott, P.J. (2014). Measuring participation outcomes following life-saving medical interventions: the Role Checklist Version 2: Quality of Performance. Disability & Rehabilitation, 36(13), 1108-1112. doi:10.3109/09638288.2013.833302

Halle, J., LeMond K., Robinson, I., Sloss R. & **Scott, P.J.** (2014). Supporting Healthy Lifestyles of Liver Transplant Candidates and Recipients. American Occupational Therapy Association 94th Annual Conference and Expo April 3-6 Baltimore, MD.

Scott, P.J. (2010). Use of the role checklist to understand habituation in recipients of organ transplantation. First International Institute on the Model of Human Occupation, Chicago, Jan 14-15.

ROLE CHECKLIST AND OSA-DLS PUBLICATIONS AND PRESENTATIONS

University of Chieti, Italy, Role Checklist Version 3 development and design of translation guidelines. April 6-8, 2019

Invitation to consult with the research faculty at the Zurich University of Applied Sciences, School of Health Professions ZHAW Institute of Occupational Therapy. Winterthur, Switzerland. March, 20-23, 2014

Scott PJ (2019) The Role Checklist Vervion 3: Psychometric and utilization with a wide variety of populations. AOTA, New Orleans April 2019

Scott P J (2019) Keynote Speaker: International Breakfast at the AOTA conference in New Orleans in April. Upcoming

Scott PJ (2019) Invited Presenter "Conversations that matter: The Role Checklist Version3: AOTA conference in New Orleans in April. Upcoming

Scott, P.J. (2018) Using the Model of Human Occupation to support translation of theory into practice: MOHO over time with practice examples from around the world. World Congress of Occupational Therapy. Cape town, South Africa, May, 2018

Scott, P.J., Fenger, K, & Vottero-Mas (2018) WFOT Participate in the translation project for the Role Checklist Version 3: A cross-culturally valid measure of participation consistent with the ICF and the Model of Human Occupation. World Congress of Occupational Therapy. Cape town, South Africa, May, 2018

Meidert, U., Bonsaksen, T., & **Scott, P.J.** (2018) Measuring Participation according to the ICF with the Revised Role Checklist. Clinical Rehabilitation. Clinical Rehabilitation 32 (11),1530-1539

Scott, P.J., Cacich, D., Keener, M., & Whiffen, K. (2017). Establishing Concurrent Validity of the Role Checklist Version 2 with the OCAIRS in Measurement of Participation: A Pilot Study. Occupational Therapy International, 2017(Article ID 6493472), 6 pages. doi:https://doi.org/10.1155/2017/6493472

Scott, P.J., McKinney, K., Perron, J., Ruff, E., and Smiley, J. (2017) Measurement of Participation: The Role Checklist v3: Satisfaction and Performance in Occupational Therapy – Occupation Focused Holistic Practice in Rehabilitation (ISBN 978-953-51-5221-7)

Kramer, J., Forsyth, K., Lavedure, P., **Scott, P.J.**, Shute, R., Maciver, D., ... in Taylor, R.R. (2017). Ch 16: Self Report Instruments. in Kielhofner's Model of Human Occupation (Fifth Edition). New York: Wolters-Kluwer.

Haglund, L., Bowyer, P., **Scott, P.J.**, and Taylor R. (2017) The Model of Human Occupation, the ICF, and the Occupational Therapy Practice Framework: Connections to Support Best Practice Around the World, in Taylor, R.R.(Ed) Kielhofner's Model of Human Occupation (Fifth Edition). New York: Wolters-Kluwer.

Scott, P.J. (2017). Patterns of occupational participation across the lifespan: Role Checklist Version 3. 5th International Institute for the Study of the Model of Human Occupation, October 14-15

Scott, P.J. (2017). The Role Checklist Version 3 (RCv3) International Institute for the Study of the Model of Human Occupation, October 14-15

McKinney, Ruff, E., Smiley, J., Perron, J. & **Scott, P.J.** (2017) Role Checklist Version 3: Feasibility and Utility. AOTA Annual Conference & Centennial Celebration. March 30-April 2. Philadelphia

Van Antwerp, L. Crabtree, JL, & **Scott, P.J.** (2016) Translation Guidelines for the Role Checklist Version 2: Quality of Performance: Feasibility Study in Iceland and China: American Occupational Therapy Association 96th Annual Conference and Expo April 7-10 Chicago

Scott, P.J., Tom, L, Parker, H. Kuegel, A, & Hamzey, K. (2016) Client-Centered Versus Impairment-Focused Approach to Participation Outcomes Following Stroke: American Occupational Therapy Association 96th Annual Conference and Expo April 7-10 Chicago

Van Antwerp, L. Crabtree, JL, & **Scott, P.J.** (2016) Translation Guidelines for the Role Checklist Version 2: Quality of Performance: Feasibility Study in Iceland and China, erican Occupational Therapy Association 96th Annual Conference and Expo April 7-10 Chicago

Scott, P.J, Tom, L, Parker, H. Kuegel, A, & Hamzey, K. (2016) A Client-Centered Versus Impairment-Focused Approach to Participation Outcomes Following Stroke: Accepted Presentation: American Occupational Therapy Association 96th Annual Conference and Expo April 7-10 Chicago.

Meidert, U., **Scott, P.J.**, Bonsaksen, T. & Fenger, K. (2016). Symposium: The Modified Role-Checklist as a Cross-Culturally Valid Measure of Participation: feasibility of translation procedure; role examples and their association with occupational participation; role examples are used for an ICF-linkage; and scoring. COTEC – ENOTHE Congress, National University of Ireland, June 15-19

Scott, P.J. (2015). The Role Checklist Version 2: Quality of Performance: A Valid and Reliable Measure of Occupational Participation. 4th International Institute for the Study of the Model of Human Occupation, October 23-24

Haglund, L., & **Scott, P.J.** (2015). Translation Guidelines for MOHO Assessment: Role Checklist Version 2: Quality of Performance. 4th International Institute for the Study of the Model of Human Occupation, October 23-24

Bonsaksen, T. & **Scott, P.J.** (2015). Clinical Applications of the Role Checklist Version 2: Quality of Performance. 4th International Institute for the Study of the Model of Human Occupation, October 23-24

Scott, P.J. & Latham, K (2015). The Role Checklist V2: QP. Development of a Scoring System. 4th International Institute for the Study of the Model of Human Occupation, October 23-24

Cacich, D., Fulk, M., Michel, K., Whiffen, K., & **Scott, P.J.** (2015). Establishing the Concurrent Validity of the Role Checklist Version 2: Quality of Performance with the OCAIRS to Assess Participation in Post-Liver Transplant Patients. Poster. 4th International Institute for the Study of the Model of Human Occupation, October 23-24.

Scott, P.J. Bonsaksen, T. Haglund, L. Forsyth, K. & Yamada, T (2015) New Developments in a Traditional Assessment to Measure Occupational Role Participation Consistent with MOHO and the ICF. 4th International Institute for the Study of the Model of Human Occupation, October 23-24

Taylor. R., Davidson, D. Pépin, G. Forsyth K, de las Heras, C G. Tsang, H. & **Scott, P.J.** (2015) Keynote & Panel on MOHO: Impact on Global Social Issues. Keynote: 4th International Institute for the Study of the Model of Human Occupation, October 23-24

Scott, P.J., Haglund, L, & Latham, K. (2015) Interactive Sessions about Translation of The Role Checklist V2, Collaborative use in Clinical practice, and Partnerships for Stuent Research Projects. 4th International Institute for the Study of the Model of Human Occupation, October 23-24

Taylor, RR & **Scott, P.J.** (2015) Workshop 1: Use of the Tools Available to Implement MOHO in a Variety of Clinical Practice Settings. 4th International Institute for the Study of the Model of Human Occupation, October 23-24

Bonsaksen, T., Meidert, U., Schuman, D., Kvarsnes, H., Haglund, L., Prior, S.,... **Scott, P.J.** (2015). Does the Role Checklist Measure Occupational Participation? Open Journal of Occupational Therapy, 3(3), 1-12.

Aslaksen, M., **Scott, P.J.**, Haglund, L., Ellingham, B., Bonsaksen, T. (2014). Occupational Therapy Process in a Psychiatric Hospital – Using the Role Checklist Version 2: Quality of Performance. Ergoterapeuten, 4, 38-45.

Wasmuth, S., Crabtree, J., & Scott, P.J. (2014). Exploring addiction-as-occupation. British Journal of Occupational Therapy, 77(12), 605-613. doi:10.4276/030802214x14176260335264

Scott, P.J., McFadden, R., Yates, K., Baker, S., & McSoley, S. (2014). The Role Checklist Version 2: QP: Establishment of reliability and validation of electronic administration. British Journal of Occupational Therapy 77(2) 96-102

Scott, P.J., Forsyth, K., Bonsaksen, T., Haglund, L, Mentrup., C, Yamada., T. (2014). Cross-cultural Validity of the Role Checklist V2: QP. Implication for an international measure of Participation. World Congress of Occupational Therapy, Yokohama Japan, June

Scott, P.J. (2014). The Role Checklist Version 2: Quality of Performance: An Outcome Measure To Reflect Improved Performance Over Time. American Occupational Therapy Association 94th Annual Conference and Expo April 3-6 Baltimore, MD.

Scott, P.J. (2012).Use of the Role Checklist as a guide to the measurement and understanding of narrative. Third International Institute on the Model of Human Occupation, Stockholm, Sweden, October 11-12, 2012.

Scott, P.J. (2012).Use of the Role Checklist as a guide to the measurement and understanding of narrative. Third International Institute on the Model of Human Occupation, Stockholm, Sweden, October 11-12, 2012.

Scott, P.J. (2011 Scott, P.J., McKinney, K., Perron, J., Ruff, E., & Smiley, J. (2018) Measurement of Participation: Utility, Feasibility, and Test-Retest Reliability of the Role Checklist Version 3. Occupational Therapy Journal of Research 39 (1) 56-63

RESILIENCE